A Sister to
Scheherazade

# A Sister to Scheherazade

Assia Djebar

*Translated by*
Dorothy S. Blair

Heinemann
Portsmouth, NH

Heinemann
A division of Reed Elsevier, Inc.
361 Hanover Street   Portsmouth, New Hampshire  03801-3912
*Offices and agents throughout the world*

*A Sister to Scheherazade*
is the second volume of a quartet.
The first volume is
*Fantasia: An Algerian Cavalcade*

First U.S. Printing 1993
First Published in English by Quartet Books Limited
A Member of the Namara Group
27/29 Goodge Street, London W1P 1FD
First published in France by Editions Jean-Claude Lattès 1987

**Library of Congress Cataloging–in–Publication Data**
Djebar, Assia, 1936–
  [Ombre sultane.  English]
  A Sister to Scheherazade / Assia Djebar ; translated by Dorothy S.
Blair.
    p.  cm.
  Sequel to: Fantasia, an Algerian cavalcade.
  ISBN 0–435–08622–7
  1. Women—Algeria—Fiction.  I. Title.
PQ3989.2.D570413  1993
843—dc20                                      92–42699
                                                  CIP

Typeset by MC Typeset Limited, Chatham, Kent
Printed in the United States of America on acid-free paper
01  02  03  04  VP  7  6  5  4

# CONTENTS

# GLOSSARY

*babouche* .............. a Turkish or Oriental slipper

*baraka* ................ Arabic word meaning blessing, good fortune or
luck

*douar* .................. a small hamlet or settlement

*fellah* ................. a peasant

*fqih* ..................... a Muslim holy man

*galette* ................ a type of pancake, made from flour, eggs and
butter, cooked under the ashes or on top of the
stove

*haïk* .................... the all-enveloping, heavy, woollen, square of
cloth in which Middle Eastern women cover
themselves out of doors, leaving only one eye
visible

*hammam* ............. Arabic word for a bath, here a Turkish bath

*medersa*
(or *madrasa*) ........ a Quranic school

*medina* ................ in Arab countries, the old part of the city, as
opposed to the modern districts

*nay* ..................... a very old species of flute

*Roumi* .................. a pejorative term applied to Europeans in North
Africa

*saroual*
(or *seroual*) .......... loose, baggy trousers

*shahada* ............... profession of faith

*sufi* ..................... a Muslim ascetic or mystic

terrace ............... in this context the French word *terrasse* refers to
the flat roof of the house, where the women
congregate for social gatherings or to sit in the
cool

*wadi* .................... a ravine or valley which becomes a watercourse
in the rainy season

*zaouïa* ................. headquarters of Islamic brotherhood, sometimes
simply a mosque

*Zitouna* ............... the Islamic university of Tunis

*'Never did the light seem so beautiful to me.'*
PIERRE BONNARD, *1946*

A shadow and a sultan's bride; a shadow behind the sultan's bride.

Two women: two wives: Hajila and Isma. The scenario of my story features a strange duet: two women who are not sisters, not even rivals, although – as one of them knows, while the other is unaware – they are both the wives of the same man – The Man – to echo the words that are murmured in Arabic dialect in the bedroom . . . This man does not come between them, but nevertheless does not turn them into accomplices.

One of these women, Isma, singled out the other to fling her into the marital bed. She had decided to act as matchmaker to her own husband; thinking naïvely to free herself by this means from her own past – enslaved to passionate love – and from the stalemate of the present. Her voice can be heard amid the play of light and dark, alternately addressing Hajila, who is before us now, and then herself, the Isma of former days . . . A voice that rings out clearly in the night, and is veiled in despair in the dazzling light of day.

Isma, Hajila: an arabesque of intertwining names. Which of the two is the shadow who will become the sultan's bride? Which one is to be the bride at dawn, only to dissolve into a shadow before noon? Scarcely has the plot started to unfold than it slowly disintegrates.

Did I intend to offer you up as a sacrifice to the man? Did I intend to model myself on the queens of the harem? These, by presenting a new bride to their master, were in fact liberating themselves at the expense of a pseudo rival . . . Was I, in my turn, reaffirming my power? No, I was cutting myself adrift. To be sure, you were the innocent victim whom I enslaved, from the day when, according to Tradition, your mother became my ally or my accomplice.

I am about to take my departure; but for the moment I am still hovering around. I speak to you as if I had known you intimately, and in so doing suppress the hint of remorse that haunts me, as if I had fallen again under the spell of those women of long ago . . .

'Hajila!'

That morning, Meriem, my six-year-old daughter, called out your name. She clung tightly to my hand and called your name for the first time out in the street. I heard the name, 'Hajila', vibrate in the blue violence of the summer morning, the name that I had so often murmured to myself when alone.

Meriem called out your name at daybreak, Hajila. And you were shaking with laughter, tossing your hair and jerking spasmodically as if racked by unwonted pain. You were descending the steps of that narrow street that we thought was a blind alley: you walked on down, ignoring the cry of your name. Gradually your long black hair ceased tossing from side to side. Other women, white-shrouded wraiths, seemed to float behind you. Children's shouts could be heard in the distance. I imagined you rushing headlong down into the town or climbing back up those countless steps. As if your future was taking shape right there, under my eyes. And so, I was able to leave you.

That same day, Meriem and I left the dusty white metropolis; we had decided to return to our childhood haunts.

'Hajila!'

My daughter repeated your name, more softly; we were approaching the Roman ruins of my native town, huddled around its ancient port, now half submerged. And back there, in the capital, you were adrift, wandering about like a beggar-woman, or maybe one who is offered for the day to passers-by or to be exposed henceforth to the sunlight, while I am tempted to plunge back into the night.

There has been no real communication between us, either by word or gesture. We have avoided any confrontation and scarcely spoken a word until that final act of the drama, when we sat side by side in the *hammam*, while the water which flowed over the paving stones at our feet, or rose in steam from the basins of the fountains, became the symbol of a truce or, maybe, of disappearance.

Have we reversed our roles? I cannot tell. Your mother and my daughter are waiting. Can we hope that the age-old burden of oppression that is our legacy may finally become the sport of wind and waves?

Your hopeless laughter at dawn, Hajila, after my daughter had called your name over the balustrade. On the blurred horizon, dawn darts its threatening eye at us. And the harbour, down below, swells with the sounds of men.

# PART I

## EVERY WOMAN'S NAME IS 'WOUND'

*'Around the house: high windowless walls surmounted by broken glass; around the village: every kind of natural protection, ditches, hedges of prickly pear; around the tent: a pack of half-wild dogs, but – rendered even more impregnable than by the dogs – the whole vicinity has been "sacralized" and cannot be violated without violating that most sacred of all concepts:* horma – *honour.'*

GERMAINE TILLION
*The Harem and Its Cousins, 1966*

# 1

# HAJILA

This morning, Hajila, as you stand in the kitchen which is to be the setting for the drama, you are suddenly, for no reason, overcome by grief. You are clearing the table on which breakfast has been served. Your eyes grow dim. You sniffle. Your fingers, suddenly out of control, chip a cup against the porcelain sink. The door of the lift on the landing slams shut; the children have left for school. You fold the tablecloth, wipe the light wooden surface of the table; you put down the damp cloth, look at your empty hands, the hands of a busy housewife. You look in the little mirror near the window and pat your cheeks; could your face be that of another woman? You dab your feverish forehead with cold water. You murmur the name of God three times, to breathe more easily: 'God the Protector, the Merciful, the . . .'

The man is looking in a wardrobe for his shirt, you can hear him somewhere behind you, without looking round. The sound of his cough in the bathroom. The cold water tap in the sink is still running. You turn off the tap. Your arms are bare. You realize you are cold. Your eyes have filled with tears. You drop your crumpled lacy handkerchief. You slowly stoop and pick it up. Then you run the hot water to wash the cups and the blue coffee-pot. Prolonged splashing in the sink mingles with the noise of the shower which you can hear through the half-open door along the spotless corridor. You whisper mechanically:

'In the name of God . . . peace and salvation!'

You are still in the grip of the same inexplicable grief. You are imprisoned by these bare walls. Tears run down your delicate, brown face; a slanting sunbeam dispels the greyness all around. But you are oppressed beneath a drizzle of melancholy:

'In the name of . . .'

You search for the name of a friendly saint. Oh, to return to the peace of former times! You close your eyes, you can't find the words, what words ... As the morning light grows brighter, you grope as in the dark, you cannot understand what is tormenting you: voices of all those female ancestors, calling on dead saints, all male corpses, every one! The tap is still running. The sun shimmers on the nearby wall. Your tears start up again, dripping into the sink, on to the sparkling floor. You stoop down ('Oh, to be able to pick up the crumbs of my shattered face, to be able to vomit out my soul! . . . O, Sidi Adberahmane of the double grave!'). You try to console yourself: 'I have not wept for so many years! Have I even prayed? The others . . . my mother, my sister, the man's children, they all recede. Only the noise that the man makes . . .'

'What's the mattter with you?'

His sharp voice is heard across the distance between you. 'He' is standing in the doorway close by.

'I'm crying!' you reply without turning round. You wait. No echo. There is no one in the room now: 'he' has gone. You hear the regular squeak of his shoes on the tiled floor. 'He' coughs; 'he' opens doors; 'he' has gone.

If only you could go on talking softly to yourself, searching through your sighs for each correct, hesitant word.

'He' has really gone. Praise be to God and to his Prophet! A sweet silence unfolds around you. The door has slammed – shattering the crystal silence of the morning. Your hand lies motionless. Let the tap run. Listen to the sound of the water dripping . . . A hand is poised on the brass tap: 'your' hand. A brow rests against a bare outstretched arm: 'your' brow, 'your' arm. You must live through the period of waiting, become a hollow, empty vessel. Children's voices rise up from the street, and reach you through the french window, across the balcony. The dawn is banished.

You stand there, a white silhouette, in front of the white sink. You swing round. You remind yourself that your name, Hajila, means 'little quail'. You pronounce the name 'Hajila' very distinctly, seeing yourself as a dirty-white bird, shivering in front of salt lakes on the horizon. Your movements are jerky, your arms thin, your legs rise up from the tips of your pink satin mules. The man has really gone out; the man, all men!

'You who can all go forth into the sunshine! Every morning, you splash water over your face, neck and arms. These are not the ablutions preparatory to prostrating yourself in prayer; no, they are a preparation for the act of leaving the house. Oh, to be able to leave the house! Once you have put on your suits, knotted your ties, you can cross the threshold, every threshold. The street awaits you . . . You can present yourself to the world, you fortunate males! Every morning of every day, you can convey your bodies into the dazzling light, every day that Allah creates! . . .'

These words throb in your head to the beat of a funeral dirge! Once the man has gone, the bedrooms are no longer empty: they are filled with sheets of translucid air. You move slowly to and fro through the apartment. The open windows seem to beckon you. One of the closed shutters, above a mattress covered in a light-coloured sheet, seems to bar your way: you step forward. Your hand strikes against the glass pane.

You walk to the bed. You make it without shaking out the sheets. It is an effort to move your arms. You sit down, stroking the counterpane of coarse, unbleached calico with fingers still bearing faint red stains of henna.

An hour later, you go and sit in the smallest of the bedrooms. Still-life with seated woman. You sit passively on a pale green rustic chair. Already, the room is flooded by so much light that streams in, wrapping you in a cloak of gold. The heat grows stronger, licking your knees; your blue printed skirt is folded back over your lap. Once again your face is flooded with tears. You lift your chin. How do you learn to rid yourself of suffering with every breath you exhale?

Down in the street, a glazier sings monotonously, then moves away into the distance, accompanied by his voice. A fly buzzes in the renewed silence; or is it a wasp? You raise your arm. You rub your right cheek with the palm of your hand. You wipe your damp cheeks. You move your hand as if you were blind.

Oh, to weep inwardly, shedding no tears! The silence slowly spills over, like a goblet full to overflowing. 'The face of sorrow,' you murmur to yourself in Arabic, to your solitary, mute self. You pass your hand over your face, feeling your prominent cheekbones, your deep-set eyes, your slightly bulging brow which softens your gaze – what gaze? of what stranger?

9

You stand up. You wear your memories, like a shawl of dust, draped over your shoulders. The day stretches out before you; no sign of wind. You close all the windows. The drawing-room blind slides down with a squeak. The darkened rooms seem inhabited; you imagine you can hear whispers, voices creeping insidiously past you, fragments of tears. What sinister ceremonial haunts these newly-whitened walls?

And you fall asleep.

It is four o'clock in the afternoon. The liftdoor on your floor clicks; steps are heard on the landing. The man's children come in: Meriem, the girl, followed by the little boy, Nazim. He is nine at the most; his sister, a little younger, has the serious expression of a woman. What unknown woman is the mother of these children? You often wonder about this, but with a passive curiosity.

They have dropped their satchels in the vestibule. You walk unsteadily towards the kitchen. You turn on the tap. This is the time when so many odours overlap: the smell of toasting bread, the coffee which you pour, the sickly breath of the approaching evening. Then you wash the cups. Your hands are busy in the sink.

'It's sunny outside, you know.'

Behind you, Meriem has spoken to her brother.

'You're crying, maman, that's not nice!' Nazim whispers in your ear.

He speaks French, like his sister; you think you can understand what he says. If the boy had been alone, he would have come to sit on your lap.

Oh, to stifle your sorrow this evening, in the kitchen which will be the setting for the drama.

# 2

# ISMA

O memory! I am standing in broad daylight; my eyes are closed but behind me, out of the heart of darkness, a flutter of wings can be heard in the dovecote. O memory! summer days or rainy days, I saunter through the streets of some capital city; sometimes long dresses are the fashion, my slightest movement becomes a dance, my skirts – copper-coloured, white, pale blue, like the eyes of the man who is waiting for me – flapping against my calves; sometimes, when legs go bare and skirts scarcely cover the knees, and my dress fits tight over my breasts, I know that my figure is trim, I am conscious of my narrow waist emphasized by my leather belt, as I quicken my steps and suddenly turn my slender neck and catch his eyes slowly studying my profile, innocent of make-up, O! this sunshine, these walks, my body sailing along – time and time again, I find myself floating in a sea of eyes, all staring at me.

To be able to bite into an apple, rush headlong down the stairs, humming a tune as I go, run recklessly across a city street without looking where I'm going, a taxi-driver, in Paris – why not in Paris! – whistles admiringly at me, coffee scalds my throat as I sit dreaming on the terrace of a brasserie, the stream of cars comes to a halt, starts up again with a screech of tyres on the damp road, while I begin to talk at random – about the dead leaves that whirl around in the November sky, about anything that comes into my head, a visit, some common or garden problem, a moment ago I thought I was in a hurry, I arrive late, the friend is waiting, looking abstracted, his thoughts elsewhere, his face a blank, seemingly indifferent as I appear, a slight irritation in his voice. 'Really, you're always late!' Each period of waiting divided by a succession of streets, by veils of mist between us. The world resumes its ordered structure only when the couple is face to face.

At twenty: adolescence scarce behind me, the days stand still, their passage barely perceptible, I emerge from a Metro station, jump into a bus, come out of a railway station, walk tall along the boulevard; at thirty, my silhouette unchanged, my eyes more eager, the calm waters of each dawn slip by, the hours the couple spend together are a rich, fertile soil; at forty, I stare anxiously at the reflection of my face in which every second of a life has left its mark, now I pause from time to time as I walk through the narrow streets, the longing in the eyes is more in evidence, the vault of the sky recedes, dove-grey, my eyes open wide: my love comes towards me, dressed in black, and I smile because we are equally heedless of Time.

I remember, oh yes, I remember so many years, a whole lifetime in a twinkling of an eye! I walk on. I remember the passage of so many days, one day succeeding another, some falling, some taking wing, without music, music sparkles in our eyes; our hands reach out to each other and the couple embraces.

A lifetime, in the twinkling of an eye. Dazzled, I spread this life out before me, already destroying it, darkening its dawns, filtering its lazy afternoons, extinguishing its sunshine, faint or dazzling – what matter! I choose only to awaken the nights: from the crest of twenty years of age, down to the valley of my thirties, through the narrow gorge of the forties, who can tell on what sky the corridor will open out? I no longer have a face or possess a veil; 'Isma', I scatter my name, all names, in a dust of snuffed-out stars.

Oh! to gather up one or other of my nights by the handful, a thousand of them perhaps; to re-create my past, our past together and all the spells we cast.

# 3

# OUT OF DOORS

Hajila, this modern apartment has been your home for six months now. The first day you came to see it with your mother, both full of respect for these long, empty rooms.

'The furniture will be delivered tomorrow,' the concierge announced. His massive form filled the corridor where he stood.

When he left, with his bunch of keys jangling on his belt, you made a thorough tour of inspection, trotting from room to room, conversing in hushed tones. Old Touma led the way, and you, Hajila, followed obediently behind. Neither of you went near the windows.

'The seventh floor, you never know! . . . May misfortune remain below! A curse on Satan!' Touma muttered.

You examined the bathroom, running your finger round the pink marble bathtub. ('I've never seen marble this colour!' you ventured, laughing shyly, like a little girl.) You sized up the lavatory – also with walls of pink ceramic tiles – then the bedrooms, and finally the two living-rooms, divided by an extraordinary glass partition. When the concierge returned he pointed out to the mother how 'chic' – that's the word he used – the place was: you simply press a red button at the side and the whole partition slides back with a sensuous swish. The two rooms were joined into one enormous salon!

Touma did not seem impressed. Worried, rather. She shrugged.

'If there are women on one side and men on the other – I'm thinking about my daughter, Hajila, when she's entertaining' (she bent her head, frowning solemnly) – 'what will be the good of that? . . . How can one protect one's . . . one's modesty?' she concluded in a whisper.

'That's a point!' the concierge admitted.

In the lift Touma went into ecstasies over the number of fitted cupboards in the corridor and the curious heating system – warm air, according to the concierge, was supposed to circulate in the ceiling! That remained to be seen! . . . As for the kitchen.

'The kitchen!'

Back in the midst of the assembled family she was moved to tears. 'I've never seen such an enormous kitchen! Oh, what bliss for my Hajila!'

She had sat there, on the only chair, facing the sink, and had declared, 'You'll be able to give them their meals there . . .'

She described the sink, the cupboards, the fitted cabinets with storage space, the balcony . . . everything! while her other daughter Kenza, her son Nasser, and even the old deaf uncle all listened.

'When I come to visit you' – she corrected herself, 'if I come to visit you, I shan't ask for anything better! You can serve my food in that kitchen! But on the floor! You've got plenty of room. But you'll have to put a low table in at the side, in addition to that high "French" table. If only for your poor uncle's sake! If he came to visit you, how could you expect him to eat, perched up so high, in his "Turkish" trousers?'

She laughed good-humouredly. The whole family was excited at the forthcoming wedding arranged so hurriedly, as soon as this unforeseen suitor had introduced himself on his return from a long period spent abroad. A widower or divorced, with two children, from one wife or two, how could they find out? who was going to inquire? 'My daughter will have room for everything in that kitchen!' Touma concluded. 'Truly blessed be Hajila, my first-born, so aptly named! When I expressed the wish on the day of her birth that she would find herself in Paradise one day, I could never have imagined such a home. Marble and glass! Blessed be the beloved Prophet for having answered my prayers!'

During this first visit, after you had both finished inspecting the kitchen, you had ventured alone on to the balcony. The view that stretched out before you had taken your breath away, with the contrasting light, the extravagant colours which seemed to dissolve under the steady glare of the sky: on the one side lay the sea, a shred verging on purple, then stripes of dark green, marked the terraces of the newly whitewashed houses; in the distance a pink brick minaret glowed with multicoloured lights.

Behind her, Touma was continuing her commentary. The

concierge returned and slid the partition back into place. You went on staring at the view, blinded by the dazzling, unchanging light. To look out over the town for the very first time, not feeling any more like a grain of dust in one of the world's dungeons, or some vermin lurking in a corner, not to have to ... Would you finally find a reprieve, there, at that window, from the turmoil to which you had been a prey since childhood?

Ten days later, dressed in new clothes, you move into the apartment which is henceforth to be your home. The husband is accompanied by his two children whom he has collected from the airport that same day. He opens the door, letting you lead the way: a queen – with the man and the children forming her retinue.

The entrance to the apartment is cluttered up with suitcases. Your own possessions, brought over the previous evening by your mother, in the lacquered trunk, have already been put away in the huge wardrobe.

You simply take off your white taffeta veil and fold it carefully. After a moment's hesitation, you put it down on a chair, as if you were going out again.

In the end bedroom, a mattress has been put down on the thick woollen Berber carpet, with its brown and white pattern. The man must have spent the last two or three nights here: crumpled sheets, cigarette ash spilt near the pillow.

You open the window to air the room. A thought takes shape in your mind, as clear as an actual memory: the two children could have been conceived here; perhaps an unknown woman, who could have been your double, gave birth here, some years ago, in this vast, desolate apartment.

Twin beds have been installed in the adjacent room. Meriem and Nazim stand and watch you bustling around: you turn the mattresses, straighten the covers, arrange the pillows on which you have put hand-embroidered pillow-cases that form part of the trousseau which you and your sister had been preparing for years. When you leave the room, the children start chattering together again, their light-hearted voices following you out into the hall.

The kitchen is packed with furniture that Touma has not seen yet: a high table, four chairs, an enormous refrigerator. She will cross-examine you later. She won't come to visit you again during the first month.

She tries to telephone you on the days she goes to look after the German's house. But you refuse to go near the spluttering apparatus. You let it ring shrilly several times before the place is plunged in silence again. You don't know what's going on; you don't want to know!

During the next few weeks, when the husband drove you over a couple of times to visit your family, you answered their questions in monosyllables. Your young sister, Kenza, wanted to know how big the fridge was, what was the make, whether you could get ice ready cut up in little pieces, if there was a special place for eggs and bottles ... 'And the low table?' Touma pestered, 'Haven't you asked "him" yet to buy it for you? What else do you still need? ...'

'Yes.' ... 'No.' ... Peace ... Silence ... Praise be to the All-Highest! The car's hooter sounded at the end of the alley where he had stopped the car because of the pot-holes. The neighbours' little girls, bright-eyed, red hair all tangled, ran to call you: 'Hurry up, Hajila! "He" is waiting for you!'

In spite of the imposing 'He', you took your time getting ready to leave; you had gone back to your everyday veil of unbleached wool; but you had changed your style: you draped yourself now in the veil in two stages, as if you'd been a town-dweller all your life, first casually flinging it round you, then, holding it firmly with one hand, adjusting it with a slow movement of your head and shoulders. It is true you were now wearing high heels – the patent-leather shoes which you'd got for your wedding; to conceal your unsteadiness you slid your feet along the ground in a graceful manner. You bent forward slightly from the waist. As you walked to the car you could feel the admiring eyes of all the women in the street, peering at you from their half-closed doors.

The black car was surrounded by a crowd of whispering urchins. You got in, clutching beneath your chin the triangle of white embroidered muslin stretched across the bridge of your nose. The car started. You lowered your eyes; the muddy alley-ways of the neighbourhood where you had spent your childhood were left behind. As soon as you were back at the 'other place', even while you were getting into the lift, you removed your veil. You instinctively counted the floors: 'sixth, seventh' ... Once in the man's apartment, you shook out your *haïk* and put it away in the same cupboard as on the first occasion.

The children had stayed behind and had already gone to bed without their supper. Under his breath, Nazim was recounting the next episode of a long serial, while Meriem stifled loud, dramatic sighs with the sheet pulled up over her eyes. They grew silent as soon as they heard their father's steps in the hall.

Whenever you returned from these excursions the kitchen seemed colder than ever. You would linger in the children's bedroom, sitting between the two beds. Nazim would promptly begin his story again for your benefit. You'd have liked to lie down on the floor between them and go to sleep right there.

The husband would cough: the indication for you to bring him an ashtray. You would enter that bedroom. There was a new bed, made of mahogany like the wardrobe. It was too high for you; like a throne? or a platform? You would lie down, next to that other body. Careful not to brush against anything. A hand would fondle your breasts in the darkness, and you would try to draw in your stomach to avoid his groping fingers . . . You would hold your breath, lying quite still, waiting, wide awake. A little later, you would get up in the dark and go to lie on the mattress on the carpet at the foot of the modern bed.

When you finally fell asleep, you could realize your dream of being spirited away – not to the shantytown, not to that slum room where your mother and sister were sleeping huddled together at that moment, while your brother and the old uncle would be lying up against the front door . . . No, somewhere far away, where you'd wandered into a cavern, 'a fluttering quail' as your mother would have said . . . or lost in the murky depths of some ocean.

It had all begun three months before; about three months prior to the drama. The first time that you had slipped out secretly.

Was it because of the baby which you had not had? That you will never have? During all that time your mother never ceased nagging you. She came to visit you now, not often, it is true, and never staying long, on her way home from looking after the German's house.

'Ask "him" to take you to see a doctor! Don't wait till it's too late!'

Why 'too late', you were about to retort. But you didn't answer. How could you tell her that 'he' was responsible? You had finally confessed to Kenza, 'I think he's "knotted"!'

'Knotted?' the girl exclaimed.

'I'm still a virgin,' you were going to add, but held back the admission. Your sister is so young. You wouldn't want to upset her. Words must spare innocence; sometimes they strike to the heart.

Touma was moaning as usual: 'Oh Sidi Abdelkader el-Jilani! You have given me idiots for daughters! They've got no sense at all! Oh, my beloved! wretched that I am!'

You gave an embarrassed, crooked smile. You twisted a heavy lock of hair around your finger. You listened. You said nothing.

One day, when Touma had gone, after giving voice to her habitual lament, you decided that you were going to cross that threshold soon. And alone! Wrapped in the shabby veil of unbleached wool which had been worn so often by Kenza. When she accompanied her mother to work, carrying buckets and saucepans hidden under its folds! The neighbours mustn't know!

For when the German was at home he gave dinner parties. Old Touma did all the cooking: a genuine couscous rolled out by hand, mutton dried ready for the winter and cooked in a hot, spicy sauce, with vegetables all prepared at home. The neighbours mustn't suspect! They'd have treated the mother and daughters as 'cooks', 'servants to Christians!'

Touma insisted that she had to make innumerable family visits. 'A poor lot,' she would bluster, with the bravado of the less fortunate members of a tribe. So Kenza, hidden by this veil with its worn fringes, would accompany her to the German's; and anyone wearing this veil could be taken for an old woman or a peasant. Especially when she wore slippers and thick socks on her feet.

You recalled the *haïk*, the slippers, the excitement you and your sister used to feel in sharing a secret, when you'd promised to repeat the lies Touma had invented.

That day, you took out the veil of unbleached wool, folded in four. You put it on the table in the drawing-room, that room where meals are never served, where the children are not allowed to sit, where once only the husband had entertained a business colleague.

It was as if this length of cloth helped you concoct your lie. As if the veil held your future days in its folds . . . Your escape.

18

You are 'going out' for the first time, Hajila. You are wearing slippers like an old woman, your head muffled in the heavy wool; your face completely hidden, leaving only one tiny gap exposed through which you peep to see where you are going. You enter the lift, stumbling over the folds of the heavy veil. Once you are outside, all alone, you will walk.

The black triangle of your eye darts to right and left – to the right again, then . . . You can feel your heart thumping under the woollen cloth, the grip of your hand on the veil beneath your chin suddenly slackens. Oh, to be able to let go of the material altogether, to look about you with unveiled face, to be able to throw your head back and look up at the sky, as you did when a child!

'But I forget myself, O All-Highest! I am intoxicated, O gentle Prophet! I stand still, I take a step forward, I glide through the air, I no longer feel the ground beneath my feet, I . . . O, widows of Mohammed, come to my aid!'

You break off the impassioned words of the prayer. The street slopes steeply uphill; the tall grey frontages of the buildings almost meet on the horizon. You climb on upwards. At a corner the sea comes into view. No one stands between you and its presence. A precipice swollen with anticipation; so many women before you must have come here surreptitiously to gaze at it. Your mind boggles.

Someone jostles you from behind. You stand stock still. You are blocking the way. You do not turn round. Then you step to one side; you scan the horizon. Is that the same sea, there, that you can glimpse from the kitchen balcony? At present it lies before you, at once near and extending far into the distance, like a gigantic lake.

You walk on again; now the road runs downhill. You want to reach the edge of the abyss. You are tempted to plunge down into it: to hurl yourself down and float in that infinite expanse, lifting your face to the mirrored expanse of the sky above. With open eyes and body adrift. The city would be reduced to a flickering spot in the distance, a dusty haze.

Countless swords sparkle in the blue expanse. On you walk, Hajila, borne along by the light that enfolds you, models you.

You are suddenly anxious. You have not been noticing which way

19

you are going and find yourself in one of the poorer districts of the city; you look up at the sky. A sky which leads nowhere. On one side there is an enormous, dilapidated building, a goods shed, possibly, or some disused premises . . . 'Suppose I couldn't find my way home? . . .' You struggle against the panic which is beginning to seize you; you retrace your steps, you . . .

Nearly an hour later, breathless from running as if pursued by some nightmare, you reach the building where you live. You don't pause till you are right in front of the lift; the entrance hall is too exposed.

The concierge stared at your unveiled face. He greeted you. You did not reply. You thought to yourself, first with a feeling of shame and then of humiliation, that it was wrong to return the greeting of a man out of doors.

As soon as you have closed the front door of the flat, you pant, still out of breath. In the entrance hall you fold up the woollen cloth. You put it away in the cupboard.

Shortly afterwards the children rang the bell. Meriem was humming to herself. Later, when you bent down to tuck Nazim up in bed, you could see the colour of the bar of the sea in his grey eyes; you remembered standing like a statue, draped in space all around you. At this memory, your heart beat frenziedly.

In the next room, the husband coughed. He must be lying in the mahogany bed. He's calling you to bring him the ashtray. You lie down with your body beside his body. You are careful not to brush against anything. A hand fondles your breasts in the dark . . .

# 4

# THE BEDROOM

The door has remained open; then suddenly, silently, it closes again; a peal of laughter rings out – convulsing the whole body, rippling through outstretched arms, down through bare legs to nymph's feet with wide-spread toes – and the whole body dissolves, invading the four corners of the room. The door closes noiselessly. Time stands still. Much later, after the voyage through the night and the turmoil of my dreams is over, the door gapes wide again. I lie quite still and surface into the still waters of morning. I am the tenuous link between the shot silk of the night and the metallic light of the new day.

A succession of places. It is broad daylight; the door slams. Our two bodies entwine in a languid, desperate embrace, each face buried in the other's shoulder, and our ardour is assuaged. The dark shadow that had stolen between us dissolves. The following evening: respite; the door is opened again discreetly just as we are about to switch off the lamp and draw the sheets up over us once more.

I hear the man shuffle out of the room, naked to the waist, his hair dishevelled; I am aroused again. He walks about the kitchen, turns on a tap; he takes a drink of water. I stretch voluptuously in the pleasurable anticipation of desire assuaged, the pleasure of exhausted limbs and compliant coupling. I lie back, my arms straight at my sides, offering up my exposed belly and breasts, keeping my eyes fixed on the bright blue-painted door-frame, tracing its rectangle. The door swings back again; the space between us dissolves and he is standing over my reclining body. In a flash, I freeze in anticipation.

The door is a barrier shutting out the world. Behind it all the corridors open out; people are getting up, moving about. Strands of time are woven around us, space curves about us, our hands are filled with flowers as yet unknown, unnamed.

No curtains. Did we forget at first, later ceasing to care? Curtains seen from the street, belying a cosy interior: curtains hanging with scarcely a flutter down impassive window-panes, lightly brushing a carpet. Net-curtains, shutting out the view.

In most of the places we lived in, the windows remained bare of any hangings, no net, no satin nor pleated taffeta. In most of the bedrooms we have slept in, there has been a curtain rod of tarnished bronze; some of wood. Once we bought a brass rod which sparkled in the first light of dawn; as soon as I opened my eyes, I could gaze at the mirrored gleam of gold . . . One morning our eyes met as we looked up simultaneously at the metal rod and . . . memories sprang at us – our bodies shone as we lay in its reflected light. I inquired if we really had to hang curtains.

I can't remember what the reply was. It was not important. None of the windows that subsequently faced our bed has had any curtains. We have watched the reds and golds of autumn melt into each other; on December mornings we have lain long abed, in indolent embraces; damp April mornings have sprinkled pink, lavender and lilac reflections over us. The translucent bow of the window spells seduction; we lie back again. We close our eyes.

We lie waiting once again, reverberating to every sound, like shells that echo the murmurs of the sea. Our bodies seem weightless; a neck is ivory, a shoulder opalescent, a knee grows suddenly soft, a cheekbone loses its sharpness, reduced to pulp, pupils seem to swim, linked hands move bonelessly, fuchsia nails blanch and disappear.

The window-panes stand between us and the drenching blueness of the sky. I turn my head on the pillow, feeling my lover's rough cheek, his eyes close and I concentrate again on maintaining our double image in my mind.

We are bathed in light that streams endlessly in through the bare panes. We drift gradually into slumber. Emptiness prevails.

I am sinking slowly, gliding through space. I must keep my eyes closed, shut out everything around me, except for the nearest wall. As our bodies grow slack, I collect my thoughts. The stones look on.

I am still sinking. I lean forward, one of my shoulders free, one of my arms tensed. I concentrate doggedly on each momentary posture I must adopt, making my limbs relax; I re-create the world behind my eyelashes.

We bend our heads at the first plunge. Faster and faster the beat; stampede of naked desire; suddenly ceasing. Once more the mutual quest. At the height of the ensuing blaze, I cannot shut out the glistening patches on the opposite wall. My temples throb and I feel I am clawing at the screen of dreams summoned up from my childhood.

The first time that I entered that long room, it seemed as if it awaited us to celebrate another wedding night. Not that there was around us the continuous hubbub of the wedding feast, as the bride grows weary, sitting like an idol, the cynosure of all the women's eyes. But the room had previously been scrubbed clean with water fetched from nearby springs, sheepskins scattered on the tiled floor and mattresses set out against the walls. And I felt invisible ancestors staring at us while I undressed with the awkward gestures of the newly-wed.

We had experienced a hundred, two hundred nights before this; but not one had been bathed in an atmosphere of such profound solemnity. A mother's hand had placed a lamp at the head of our bed. Wherever we were subsequently to sleep – hotel rooms, anonymous rooms – we would carry with us the glare of the whitewashed walls of this bridal chamber. The austerity of the setting betrays a secret.

'Isma, this is where I was born!' the man begins.

'The old high brass bedstead no longer exists!' the mother interrupts, not hearing the admission, but guessing what has been said.

She turns her head to me, her daughter-in-law, whom she never names.

'It was the custom . . .' this apologetically, 'the parents on the bed, the children underneath!'

'The cradle was hung under the high mattress,' the man recalls, his voice raising an echo in the long, empty room.

'Those mattresses are there for you until you bring your bedroom furniture!' the lady explains. Then she leaves.

'Of course!' I murmur dreamily.

How can I tell her that we possess neither bed nor chest of drawers nor bedside table? We shall not buy any. We shall move from place to place, sufficient in ourselves, rich or not, as may be.

In the half-light the wall seems fissured. I bring my hand out from under the blanket and feel it. The man still sleeps, his legs intertwined with mine. The piled-up mattresses which serve as our marriage bed have recently been refilled with fresh wool. I am moved by the thought that, by the coming summer, we shall have left the imprint of our embraces in the impacted wool that has been so carefully teased out. The following nights the husband pushed me up against the wall. We stayed in that house throughout a white winter.

Still half-asleep, I can hear the sounds of the women of the family outside in the courtyard, going about their morning domestic activities. I move away from my beloved. Wrap him in caresses. Uncover him – is he still sleeping? I bury my head against his shoulder, am carried away in the rising waters that flood over me. The coffee-pot is singing out there on the patio. My body stretches and flexes, my eyes remain open.

I lean against the partition to climb down from the bed; there is very little space between it and the wall. I crouch at the head of the bed, brushing the man's gleaming pupils with my breasts. I am burdened with pity, as if on the shores of this slowly dawning day, the presence still lingered of that elderly woman with the dark circles around her eyes – the woman who had murmured, 'These mattresses . . . until your bedroom furniture arrives . . .!'

That evening, my husband pushed me against the partition again. Perhaps unable to bear the clammy heat, when the wind blew incessantly from the south for three whole interminable days. Screens of dust separated objects and creatures alike; the gusts of hot air kindled vague feelings of resentment.

Nights when the air is never still, nights of unease: locks rattle, a tin can falls with a crash somewhere in a yard. Virgins open dim eyes wide, tradesmen stop snoring, toads cease their croaking. Only the rustle of the fountain persists, softly breaking the surrounding silence. The wind cuts off our room from the outside world. The walls stretch away into the distance.

Our bodies toss and turn; a cat mews on a roof; not far away, a matron groans. A brief caress and then our arms break loose from the embrace. Outside, the storm rages.

I curl up again and go off to sleep; the man's legs stretch out to find me. In the morning the wind has abated. I open my eyes, dreamily, fascinated by the whiteness of the corner facing me.

'What a night!' the housewives will sigh, when I join them. For the moment I have no desire to leave the bedroom; if only I could creep under a stone, like an insect, and forget the turmoil.

Lying with head thrown back, hair lying loose like a palm tree's whorl of foliage, neck arched towards the bed on which there is no pillow. Recent transports have left no mark on these features; that languor betrays no past sighs of passion. Might not these closed eyelids betoken the exhaustion of a body over-exerted . . .? Is it nothing but the turmoils of disturbed slumbers? Lips tremble, in a repressed sigh.

I raise slender arms and trace a vague figure in the air, then drop them again to curve around my face. In the confusion, my breasts are uncovered; a profile with waxen features appears, with beads of perspiration on the brow.

I must open my eyes: all my limbs are floating, the muscles of my back relax, my cheekbones are softly rounded, irregular samples of some potter's craft, my shoulders curve and every finger of each hand plays music for some mute odalisque.

In the centre of the ceiling the lamp swings wildly, like a fragile mark on an alabaster belly.

The man still sleeps. I gaze down at him, then I get dressed. I go to join the women-folk of the family on the patio.

# 5

# NAKED IN THE WORLD

# OUTDOORS

Hajila, a few days later you escaped for the second time. Your husband had driven you out to the shantytown, to visit your family. This time he came in with you: he had wished everyone 'well over the fast'. You saw him offer a hundred-dinar note to Nasser, your young brother, who hesitated for a moment and then stuffed it into his pocket. You looked away. The children had stayed in the car, with all the urchins of the neighbourhood swarming round them, and must have been growing impatient.

The man drove home in silence, taking a different route. Because of Meriem who had asked him something in her solemn voice, far too serious for her age. You noticed that the car slowed down in a broad street.

You turn round and look out of the back window. The scene that retreats inexorably before your eyes is of tall white buildings whose flat roofs open on to bands of metallic blue sky. You begin to feel almost giddy. You close your eyes. The man is carrying on a quiet conversation with his daughter who sits in front with him; they could be guests around a tea table. You listen to their alternating voices, punctuated by silences, to which the hum of the engine lends emphasis. You understand a few scraps of French. From the very first day, they have been shut off from you by this musical language, which they brought with them, at the same time as their luggage.

You open your eyes again. You are passing a nondescript little public garden, a bare triangle with raised benches, visible from the road. The car is held up at a crossing. You watch the traffic lights changing automatically to red. Then you turn to look at the little garden.

A woman with a push-chair has just sat down on one of the benches. She leans forward and picks up a baby; she is right in front of you. She stretches out her bare arms as if to throw the infant up in the air; this unknown woman gives a peal of uninhibited laughter, her evident delight clearly legible on her face which is framed by a halo of red hair. The baby wriggles, the woman laughs, she is just about to lower her outstretched arms when . . .

The car moves off suddenly. It turns to the right. The laughter, the baby held up in the air, the little garden, everything is suddenly lost from sight . . . You look straight ahead: the back of the man's head, the heads of Nazim and Meriem sitting beside him. You think to yourself, 'Henna-ed hair . . . She couldn't have been a French woman!' You repeat to yourself, 'Henna-ed hair . . . Not a French woman.' And you muse, 'Without a veil, out of doors, playing lovingly with her child!'

You repeat, 'Out of doors, without a veil, loving . . .'

'No veil, out of doors . . .'

The refrain continues to haunt you as you get into the lift, then enter the vestibule; the door slams behind you, while you fold your best veil in two, then into four, then eight. And you put it away.

In the kitchen Nazim implores you, 'Maman, let me stay with you! If "he" calls me, say that I'm learning Arabic!'

'Yes, my precious, may the Lord bless you!'

He smiles. He is used to the formula of these blessings. He doesn't understand them. He accepts them like glancing kisses.

He is the only one who is making any progress in the native tongue. Meriem never addresses a word to anyone except her father or brother. When you ask her what she wants while you are serving the food, she replies with a nod or a shake of her head; she deliberately looks right through you as you remain standing there, her expression one of complete indifference.

Nazim, on the other hand, has begun to repeat your words with application. He loves you. So much so that, thank God, he does not speak Arabic with his father's accent, inherited from that city on the border which he had left at least twenty years ago: an accent that makes the language sound pedantic, with emphasized dental

27

consonants and slurred gutturals. An Arabic that sounds quite different from yours, and with a peculiarity due probably to his peripatetic life – he puts everything in the masculine.

You recall the first time he addressed you – you turned round to look for the person he was speaking to: you were no more present than a ghost!

But Nazim spells out the words lovingly, with those soft intimate sibilants, such as your own people use, your mother's neighbours, and so many others. You are congratulated on Nazim's progress. You accept the compliments modestly; the husband nods his approval and stares long at you. So the reason for your presence in this place is confirmed: without your realizing it, you were chosen as a governess, 'Miss Hajila'.

The unknown red-head was laughing! You had not been able to hear her through the closed window of the car. The dinner is simmering on the stove; Nazim follows you from the sink to the table. He puts out the dishes, sets each place, names every object in Arabic; you are engrossed in the patient game; you think to yourself that, outside these walls, the woman is still laughing.

'Henna-ed hair . . . She wasn't French!'

You are haunted by these words, while you serve the three sitting round the table. When they've gone, you hurriedly eat without bothering to sit; you think, 'I just make a pretence of eating! . . .' You can't swallow anything else. You slump into a chair. You take your time doing the washing-up, dusting, polishing. Nazim appears noiselessly, barefoot, whispering from the doorway, 'Mma! . . . come! . . . What about my story?'

You smile.

'Henna-ed hair . . . No veil, out of doors!'

As you continue to dwell on the memory of the little public garden, you become aware that you have made an irrevocable decision: 'Tomorrow, I shall do it again!'

When, crouching down by the children, you hear the man calling, asking for an ashtray, waiting, you go to him, you let him touch you, making yourself as small as possible. And as soon as you can slip away, you lie down on the mattress on the floor and lull yourself to sleep with the sweet, consoling words: 'Tomorrow, I shall do it again!'

You sink down into the darkness where the vision of the

unknown red-head appears before your eyes, seated in the little garden, her face radiant with joy.

As you emerge into the open, you can feel the concierge's eyes staring at your back. You hurry down the first incline of the first hill. You pause beneath a balcony to get your breath. A baby up above whines miserably; a young girl's muffled voice can be heard pleading with it – a sister perhaps, or a very young mother. Suddenly an Oriental singer's voice ripples from the depths of a room nearby:

> *A love all-embracing has been my lot*
> *in the love I have known!*
> *Time all-encompassing, so time has passed*
> *in my love*
> *for you!*

'Son of a dog, come in if you want to, I can't come out! Oh, shut up! Shut your noise!' the childish voice is heard grumbling from the balcony, while the singing is followed by the sound of violins.

You breathe normally again. Ever since you slammed the door behind you, you have been devoured by fear, as if you were escaping for the first time. You feel for a handkerchief under your veil; you dab your neck, your forehead, your cheeks. It is not hot in spite of the dazzling light. Shadows dance in the breeze on the walls. Someone, behind a blind, is warming a teapot, brewing mint tea. There is not a soul in the street; it could almost be a village footpath. The child on the balcony is quiet now; he must have gone back into the room. The voice of the singer on the radio can be heard again, softly repeating her refrain:

> *In my love . . . for you!*

Just up above, the unknown girl hums the same song in her harsh voice; she's probably the child's mother or the baby-sitter. She sings along with the voice on the radio, maybe sitting down on the tiled floor. You muse on this proximity and, feeling more at peace, you continue on your way.

You were walking in the shade; now you are in the sun. Suppose the sun's rays were to wrap around your arms, penetrate to your very armpits, suppose . . . Under the worn wool of the *haïk*, the neck of your mauve cotton dress is cut very low, with little cap sleeves just covering your shoulders; you chose it for its loose skirt that comes just to mid-calf and allows you to walk freely.

You finger the material.

You have reached a wide congested avenue, full of cars and crowded buses struggling up the hill.

'I must cross here . . . Then!'

You concentrate. Suddenly you run across to the other side. A car screeches to a halt. A man swears at you, then smiles. You don't turn round, overcome with embarrassment. You enter a narrow alley, between rows of houses with gardens surrounded by high walls. 'Afterwards! . . .'

There, you make your sudden decision to take off that veil! As if you wished to disappear . . . or explode!

After the next corner, you are tempted into a shady street that runs uphill. Suddenly, there is no traffic: as if spring were lying snugly curled up in this tiny haven of solitude. You take a few long, deep breaths. Here and there, between the rows of tall buildings, there are two or three private houses, surrounded by low walls.

At a dusty crossroads, two little boys about ten years old, in short trousers and rope-soled sandals, catch up with you. They hurry on taking no notice of you. One of them turns round for a moment, casually; the other one walks awkwardly, carrying on his head a basket covered with a cloth.

As you slow down, the woollen veil slips off your head; you try to imagine what you look like, bare-headed, your black hair drawn back. Now your long pigtail, that had been bunched up under the veil, emerges from hiding. You shrink back. Your hands reach for your neck, trembling:

'Out of doors . . . O Lord! O sweet Messenger of the Lord!'

You walk, you skip. This hawthorn hedge that suddenly appears . . . you could climb over it easily. On the other side of the street there is a ditch running along a fairly high wall: oh! to be able to look over it and satisfy a mischievous curiosity! You come to a sudden stop; with a dancer's sharp gesture, you shrug one shoulder, then the other; suddenly the woollen cloth falls about your hips, revealing your blouse. The wool of a shroud . . .

The material is now gathered round your waist. You stand still on one foot, the other poised on the tip. Your heart beats faster. Then, with your right hand, you wrench the cloth away and bundle it up, letting it drag on the ground. You take just one step forward: you stop again under a tree. You are assailed by the abundance of scents around you: the hawthorn hedge, then some wild plant that you do not recognize. You are enveloped in a profusion of smells, some sweet, some acrid, that hold you in thrall . . .

Finally your hands come to life and fold up the veil as if of their own accord: in two, in four, in eight. The pool of sunlight has spread, flooding the narrow street. In front of you, one of the two boys has reappeared; he has turned round, scarcely glancing at you: you the new woman, you who have just been transformed into another woman. He walks on; his companion, who has also now reappeared, brushes past you and walks away, whistling: he must have seen you from the back and carried your image with him, the image of your unveiling.

You tuck the *haïk* under your arm; you walk on. You are surprised to find yourself walking so easily, at one fell swoop, out into the real world!


The alley-way twists and turns. With your free hand you pat the back of your neck, making sure that the slide is holding the long plait firmly in place . . . You are determined not to hurry, now that you are going to present yourself to the eyes of so many strangers, all those whom the Lord sets in your path!

A little further on, a long queue is standing outside a shop which appears to be shut, although the metal blinds over the windows are not down. Will all these passive, patient people, men and children, standing stock-still waiting, like so many Peeping Toms, become suspicious as you approach and be prepared to give evidence against you? 'Shall I ever manage to walk past them? How shall I ever dare? Oh, Messenger of the Lord . . .'

A car travelling at full speed appears at the crossroads. You pull up; you take this opportunity to cross to the other side, to avoid the row of staring eyes. 'Oh, Messenger of the Lord, where can I go, henceforth?' 'Out of doors . . . naked!'

31

In your agitation you overshoot the point where the main roads meet. You hastily run through the list of all the people who might have recognized you if they happened to be in that queue. Might they have been waiting to buy semolina, or condensed milk? . . . You try to stifle your panic.

'The men of my family, my uncle, my brother, the three cousins on my father's side who come to town once a year from their farm in the country, they would all turn their eyes away respectfully, saying that my husband had made me leave off the veil!'

You rack your brains.

'On "His" side, who knows me? . . . Any children? Any relatives? No, he's the only one!'

You give a little giggle.

'Him? . . . Naked, I am Hajila, stripped naked!'

You throw back your head, like the woman yesterday in the little public garden . . . You would like to find her again. Which way should you go? To find your way, you'd have to remember exactly . . . What could you remember? You turn to the right, then to the left; you are still in a maze of narrow alley-ways. You avoid the boulevards, you're afraid of the cars, you recognize the hospital first. You must have come here when you were small, when your father was ill.

'To go out naked!' you think. This is a return to childhood! O black rock of Mecca!

You feel you are going to suffocate! . . . It is only excitement.


You reach an oasis of green; it is not the little park you had seen from the car yesterday, but a genuine garden with terrace rising upon terrace. You enter, overwhelmed with amazement. Flowering hedges, winding white gravel paths, benches inviting you to sit in shrubberies, flights of steps with climbing roses rioting over their balustrades: a fit setting for a bride. This is how other people live in foreign countries, according to the television!

A couple are sitting in a corner. The girl is veiled; she half turns round keeping her face lowered, but uncovered. She is wearing violent make-up on her eyes and mouth. The man puts his arm round her shoulders and whispers to her, as if giving her some instructions. The girl's kohl-rimmed eyes glance at you, absentmindedly. You walk away: you are the passer-by today!

You see yourself walking with the eyes of the veiled girl upon you. You turn down another path. You'd like to be able to sit. To gaze at the city stretched out at your feet, the sea a horizontal strip on the horizon, like yesterday. You find a seat, in the shade of a cedar. People are walking about: one group, followed by two or three others. You're like a posed photograph mounted in an album. On glossy paper. You can't be seen very clearly against the tree behind: or so you hope. You cannot look. You dare not look. You sit rigid. You do not lower your eyes. You gaze out towards where the horizon should be. A clump of geraniums blocks your view. Nothing happens. Your veil lies in a crumpled heap on your lap; you clasp your hands tightly together, as if for some ceremony in which no guest may move.

An old man walks past; his robe an immaculate white; a rosary in his quivering fingers which brush you as he passes, betraying a weakness or some infirmity. You shudder at the gleam in those senile eyes which soon retreat into the distance. Another silhouette approaches; is there to be an endless procession of men? Are they all to scrutinize you with their piercing eyes?

You stand up; you regret your action immediately, but it is too late. You must try to find another bench, in another path! There's nothing. You'll have to start walking again. Once out of doors, the only thing you can do is keep walking: you don't stroll along, you don't run, you don't flop down on the ground. At least if you'd kept your veil on, you could crouch down; the men would see a white heap on the ground. You can't laugh like the woman yesterday. She was holding a baby in her arms. She had a baby's pram. Your imagination races feverishly: 'If I had a baby, would the man let me take it out as far as the little public garden? I would be able to laugh, I would be able to forget: an unknown woman prisoner, passing in a car, would envy me! . . . I haven't got henna-ed hair, but . . .'

When you leave the park, you decide to walk back along the boulevard. You will find the way. Must you go back yet? The daylight lingers on, the day seems endless. Then the light begins to fade. The wind has slackened to a light breeze. It blows up the dust. The streets are filled with endless crowds. You climb the hill. You will walk for hours, you will struggle on, you'll find the way.

After many long minutes, you remember the address where you

live: it's a residential district in the upper part of the town. You have only one recourse if you are to find your way back: you furtively enter the dark hall of a building; with trembling hands, your face contorted in despair, your eyes closed, creating the darkness that reflects your own dark misery, you wrap yourself once more in the *haïk*! You emerge into the street, a ghostly figure once more, and under the white veil grey anger folds up its wings.

You clutch the woollen cloth tightly to adjust the tiny triangle that leaves your one eye uncovered. Now that you are anonymous once more, you find your voice to mutter mild imprecations, in your resentment calling down curses on everyone, including yourself, cursing your life . . . You hail a youngster who is passing. In a gruff voice, you give the address where the Man lives. The lad points out the way you must go. He's about to walk away; suddenly, wanting to be helpful, possibly guessing at your distress, he adds, 'Yes, you've got another ten minutes' climb, but there's a bus, if you prefer!'

'Thank you, my son!'

Muffled in the folds of the veil, you bless him.

Your despair is suddenly lifted as you laugh at the idea that every veiled woman has one father, one husband, but many, many sons! All these men, out in the street, 'All my sons!' You are surprised to find yourself searching for insults, obscenities, you who, only a few months before, condemned the coarse language of the women in your neighbourhood!

'May the widows of the Prophet preserve me! May the Sainted Rabéa intercede for me in the life hereafter! May I be cursed! May I be possessed by misfortune with the wrinkled monkey face! May the white-draped widows protect me! May all the perfumes of the Kaaba form a halo around me! May . . .'


Half an hour later, you are passing the concierge with bent head. You stand quite still in front of the lift which is slow in coming. Behind you, the concierge is summing you up. He notices the crumpled veil wrapped around you; he imagines you have been to a secret tryst, pictures your amorous embraces. Perhaps, he thinks, you sell yourself!

As you go up in the lift, you uncover your face. The woollen cloth slips down over your shoulders. When the front door of the apartment closes behind you, you do not put the cloth back in the cupboard. You drop down on to the mattress, on the floor in the bedroom, still bundled up in your shroud.

Then you go to the bathroom. You undress and lie down in the steaming bath. You study your body in the mirror, your mind filled with images from outdoors, the light from outdoors, the garden-like-on-the-television. The others are still walking about there; you conjure them up in the water reflected in the mirror, so that they can accompany this woman who is truly naked, this new Hajila who stares back at you coldly.

# 6

# VEILS

We often go out shopping together for our clothes, waiting always till the last minute, when the need for something urgently forces us to shake off our inertia. When we've selected the coat, tried on the shoes – court or casuals? – when the nylon underwear has been wrapped, we hurry out of the shop. The following evening I preen myself in front of the mirror:

'What do you think of the cut of this jacket?'

'This material won't last; too bad!'

The qualms of possessing: moulding satin or linen to the curves and angles of one's body, or floating in billowing folds of silk. And to conclude the tableau – the flirtatious passionate embrace:

'I'd never have bought this dress by myself!'

Expressing my gratitude like a kept woman! It's only a game. I suddenly feel the urge to go out, in spite of the cold. I need to walk about aimlessly, to give free rein to this gratuitous excitement. My body moves easily in my new dress, red suits me, the sharp spring morning stings my cheeks! The memory of the preceding night spurs me on; it wraps me around in an invisible halo of gold dust. Does passion secrete an indelible stain?

'Open the wardrobe, let me choose a pullover for you!'

We clothe ourselves in coverings of flannel, crêpe or wool: we veil ourselves to face the world! Otherwise would the secret – what secret? – be destroyed?

'I don't understand!' the man insists, surprised that I don't buy any new clothes for a whole season.

I take delight in poverty ... A student's raincoat, a baggy pullover, shabby jeans, shoes that I kick off as soon as I come in. Hair scraped back off my face, offering to my sweetheart's eyes only features unadorned, a pensive gaze or furrowed brow.

In these ascetic interludes, I give up even the most routine cosmetics. I am obsessed by the need for the most basic cleanliness: I wash my face with the cheapest soap, I scrub myself from head to the soles of my feet with the harshest loofah, I let the ice-cold shower tingle relentlessly against my back – and the splendour of a new dawn is reflected in my eyes and my wet and glistening neck. I stand in front of the misted mirror, in the unlocked bathroom: I would become a nun if need be and take the veil, to let it suddenly slip down, there, before my eyes!

By day then, I am constantly on the go, exulting in the purity of youth, by night, by way of contrast, I wallow in unashamed sensuality. While, out of doors, I shroud my breasts in coarse wool, and hide ankles and wrists from view in the leather of boot or glove, once back in our room my whole body assumes its own identity again. Shoulders, arms, hips are released, obedient to the scenario of the night.

We sink into an identical languor. I, for my part, take my time, a courtesan dallying in foreplay. No precipitous haste, no urgency of passion. We exchange slow caresses. Waves of drowsiness flood over us: every part of my body seems to move independently, a breast becomes an upturned goblet, belly a receding shore, shoulders dig into the pillow, and my legs – ah, my legs! – become a diver's dream.

In the depths of the night, I sigh in my sleep. Half-awakened, my partner hears the murmur; he stretches out one hand to press me against his shoulder blades. A rider with two faces, we pursue our dreams.

When passion is sated, when we no longer need to exchange caresses, we lie hand in hand, like brother and sister, murmuring to each other just before the first light of dawn.

'We could happily die now, like this, providing that we could share the same grave!'

And I recall stretches of sand. Rural graveyards, where the people in the land of the sun put their loved ones into the earth, with no coffin, wrapped only in the first cloth to hand. Our posture foretells how we shall lie in death: heads thrown back, eyes expressionless, jaws set in a grin, we shall disintegrate.

My sweetheart turns on his side, folds me in his arms. Sleep gradually overtakes me again.

When evening returns, discarded clothes lie in a pool on the floor. I bend down, the man fixes his eyes on the flexible curve of my spine. I concentrate on my preparations for the night while, at the same time, seeing myself through the other's eyes. I straighten up, fold silk or nylon garments tidily on a chair, turn my head – the colour has scarcely faded from my face and my features will soon soften as I break adrift. I pull on a man's shirt, sit cross-legged while the man smokes. I bend my head coyly, and nostalgia creeps into the flirtatiousness that is the prelude to desire.

'The smell of mint!' I whisper some time later. 'Do you remember?'

He remembers. Leaf-mould underfoot, shreds of mist hanging from the branches of the ilex tree, one clear night. We had been driving along a corniche, taking our time over our return in a ramshackle old jalopy; we had run out of petrol and had slept in the open. When we awoke, the brilliance of the morning bursting over the undulating countryside flooded over us.

We avoided the patch of mud under the elm tree. We sat a little further away, against a rock. We only had to turn our heads to catch sight of the precipice: far in the distance, a violet patch of sea, no bigger than a pocket-handkerchief. On a slope of the hill, a shepherd was wandering with a few goats among the Roman ruins. He always greeted us with a smile these May mornings, when we lingered in this region and took our many walks. We climbed the mountain paths, and when twilight had finally faded, we went back to that abandoned hut, with the mattress on the bare earth and the white wooden table in front of the window – a window opening on to unfamiliar scents.

One night, we were overtaken in the maquis by the urgency of our desire. A smell of anemones lingered, I think, after the afternoon shower. The child was born in February. I never say 'my daughter' . . . I shall never admit how slack my body grows now and how I feel hollow inside when the father bends over the child and they both roar with laughter – he, normally placid or sad, and Meriem, fluttering like a seagull, with her inexhaustible peals of laugher. The man puts his arms round her; weakness overcomes me as I stare at the vision of them together.

The child grows bigger; her chubby limbs lengthen out. At the sight of her mobile features, her big, round, laughing eyes, I recall a woman lying on dead leaves, amid a host of persistent smells, disregarding the damp of the last days of spring . . .

A floor, of pale tiles; walls covered with mosaics in faded colours. The villa has a white façade and terraces, this space that is ours at Meriem's birth. Then we occupy a flat that is sparsely furnished, but whose windows overlook the Mediterranean. We are drenched in the cool air that filters in everywhere, as every evening I leave all the windows open, except in the child's room. Then I am regularly wakened by the cold; when I get out of bed, my sweetheart urges me, 'Don't walk barefoot, at least put your slippers on!'

'I'm going to look at Meriem, I heard her cough in her sleep!'

'You think I don't know! You want to cuddle her; you wake her up on purpose to play and laugh with her!'

'No, really, she did cough!'

I pick my daughter up, I carry her from her room to ours; I put her in our bed, between us. While she gurgles to herself – she is a very good baby, laughing when we want her to laugh, waking up when we are tired of her sleeping – we talk at length, fruitlessly, of the years before us.

# 7

# THE OTHERS

The next few days, Hajila, you drifted aimlessly about the flat. When the man had gone out and the children had left for school, you roamed from room to room, your arms stretched out in front of you, like a sleepwalker. Suppose all the furniture were to be removed, there would be much more room; suppose one made do with mattresses piled on top of each other! This drawing-room where nobody came to sit . . .

The windows remained open letting in irregular bursts of noise; and dust as well. In the kitchen the sun licked at the sink; the saucepans hanging on the walls, the gas-stove, every object seemed to be waiting for you.

You wore your mauve cotton frock again. Your hands fumbled with the buttons of the blouse and the fastening of the belt; you knew you would not be going out. Not yet!

In the evening, when his sister was out of earshot, Nazim inquired with loving concern – a secret between the two of you, 'What's wrong?'

And later, he repeated his bewildered appeal. 'What's wrong . . . Mma?'

'What could possibly be wrong, my darling, my precious?'

You no longer played your little game. The game that consisted of telling him the Arabic word for all the objects he could spot. And, at bedtime, you had to force yourself to repeat mechanically some well-worn story, as you tucked him up in bed.

When the man called from the high bed in the next room for you to bring him the ashtray, you pretended not to hear. You went out on to the kitchen balcony in the dark. Shivering in your cotton dress, you swore that the very next day you would burn the woollen veil: destroy the temptation.

On the third day you began to venture out again. After that you went out every day. You always wore your veil in the lift and when you passed the concierge, who no longer spied on you; you paused at the same spot under the balcony where the baby whimpered. You didn't remove the veil now in the footpath lined with hawthorn hedges, but further on, in the vestibule of a dark building, whose broken door was always ajar. To the right, at the first corner, the same crowds jostled at the hospital gates.

And so every day you make your escape. You become quite familiar with the little public gardens and squares of this neighbourhood. To find your way about, you recall where you went the day before, and the day before that, and so on. You have never seen the red-haired stranger again. Perhaps she's still laughing, holding her baby in her outstretched arms; perhaps she's waiting for you in that little garden.

In the evening, when you return with aching legs and the rumblings from the outside world drown the beating of your heart, you tell yourself that you too have a history.


Once out of the house, you never tire of walking; you learn to make discoveries. Objects and people dissolve into shapeless, colourless blobs. Spaces open up through which your body can pass without disturbing anything. You tell yourself that no one takes any notice of you, once you have dropped your veil: you are a stranger whom no one knows, moving freely about, with open eyes. Sometimes men stand aside to let you pass. And you sweep majestically by.

The next stage is to begin to remember certain aspects of other people's appearance, and also something of the shape of objects. Seated on a bench in a square, amid a horde of jostling, whining children, amid a throng of adults, your eye is caught by a pair of down-at-heel shoes, a flashy jacket, a hand waving a cigarette-end under your nose to emphasize a conversation being carried on above your head. Only the women – young ones, peering at you through lace veils stretched over their noses, old matrons with uncovered faces and eyelids blackened with antimony, their arms encumbered with babies or parcels – only the women have eyes for you. And you can feel their piercing gaze linger after they have passed.

Once you are out of the house you begin to be especially aware of sounds: isolated cries or outbursts that rise and fan out on the air, shreds of isolated conversation suddenly audible in a pause in the hubbub, the spells of silence which dance round you as you climb back up the avenue and begin to worry unduly about the lateness of the hour.

One day you sit down in a public garden, bolt upright, your hands folded demurely in your lap. A man whom you'd not noticed approaching is bending over to speak to you. You can't tell if he's young or old, a foreigner perhaps; you're seized with panic, you didn't hear what he said! You understand only that this face with the grey-green eyes is asking you something. There's a hair protruding from a wart at the end of the man's eyebrow. You tremble; you feel the stranger's rumblings are an attack on you. You turn your head mechanically: what are you to say? what must you do? The crooked smile hanging over you seems hesitant. The man moves off. When he reaches the end of the hedge you can see his back quite distinctly: he's wearing the conventional suit of the city-dweller and the hat of the well-dressed bourgeois. The question this man with the grey-green eyes had asked fell on empty air.

As if you were able to speak! Don't people realize that you are out of doors? The memory of the laughing woman returns. You too could listen to your own voice calling out or singing; why not? . . . But when you throw off the woollen veil, when you roam around, your voice seems to have been left behind. It catches up with you only at the very last minute, when you have wrapped the cloak around you again, just before you start to climb back home.

At that moment you are surprised to find yourself suddenly trembling with alarm. If people bump into you, you are apt to curse them in the terms used by the women of the shantytown. Is this spiteful irascibility typical of all those ghostly, white-shrouded creatures in the street? Is it their revenge? To shout insults, because one's body has taken on a leaden hue?

In the surge of emotion when the stranger addressed you, you realize you have lost the power of speech. At the same time, you feel with a curious sharpness as if your arms are bathed in warm air. A mottled flush floods over you. For these expeditions out of doors you always wear the same dress. Yesterday evening you washed it carefully before going to bed. You put on a dressing-gown. Was this while waiting for your second skin to dry?

Do women who venture out unveiled really own several frocks? Taking their time over dressing, every time they go out, deliberating over the choice of a colour, a silk, the fullness of the blouse! You muse over such wealth, this good fortune that so many unknown women enjoy, for there must be hundreds of them, and you who never envied the other guests at the weddings you used to attend – those women who wore such an accumulation of jewels on their chests! If only you could talk to some of those regal creatures today!


After a week or more you have become 'a woman who leaves the house'. When you return in the evening you are filled with the sensation of the infinity of time. As if each day were a repetition of the last; as if intimations of mortality which had previously lain coiled up inside you were beginning to ooze away, bringing on brief bouts of fever. You feel your forehead; you go out on to the balcony; you catch the last gleams of twilight in the distance. No, you are not ill. The usual work awaits you in the kitchen. The children are whispering.

Before going to bed you take refuge again on the balcony, in the dark. You crouch down on the tiles. Now only a tiny scrap of sky is visible.

You concentrate on the places you have walked through earlier that day; you imagine them too being swallowed up by the night!

In the morning the man fumes over his breakfast; he curtly demands his clean clothes. He repeatedly finds excuses to call to you from the bathroom: he can't find a towel or a piece of soap. 'The water isn't hot enough,' he complains – so many trivialities . . .

You wait impassively. At last they have all gone. The day begins: the walls seem to be closing in on you, the furniture gets in your way. You are seized by an irresistible urge to obliterate the outline of objects. The open windows are yawning chasms of blinding blue. You kneel down – no! it is not one of the five moments of prayer. You lie down on the floor, under the open window. Your eyes are filled with sky; you lie still and empty. You do not feel yourself present in that place, nor yet anywhere else; bursts of sound reach you from outside. You absorb them.

43

You grow drowsy. You do not daydream. You do not sleep, you savour this languor. And then Touma, your mother, arrives unexpectedly.

You let the bell ring for a long time. The door-knob rattled; someone was banging on the door. You got up from the floor. You opened the door; you look half-asleep. Your mother and the concierge stare at you, an unspoken question in their eyes.

'You see,' Touma shouts to the concierge, 'I told you my daughter Hajila never leaves the house!'

The door blew shut. When the concierge had gone, she resumed more quietly, 'Didn't you hear the bell? You never used to sleep so soundly before you were married!'

You let her ferret around in the flat. Eventually she settles herself in the drawing-room; this is the first time she's ever sat there. You crouch at her feet – a little girl again.

'The concierge is right, Mma . . . I do leave the house now! – You're smiling, you're pulling a face – I go out nearly every day!'

You were about to add, 'May the Lord forgive me! May . . .' But you say nothing more. Quite deliberately. You must beg for nothing, gabble no empty formula of protection! No . . .

Tears stream down Touma's face; it's the usual scene! The ritual performance!


She jumps up from the velvet armchair, sinks down on the floor, her legs apart, her *saroual* pulled up above her arthritic knees; her veil has slipped down to her shoulders. She beats her breast spasmodically with her henna-ed hands. Her fine-fringed hair – her only vanity – comes undone, she turns up her eyes, her mouth gapes open, the gold rings in her ears quake: mercilessly, you note all the details of this grotesque pantomime.

She weeps, does this mother; she drones, she mutters, she bursts into snatches of song. She stops only when she needs to draw breath, punctuating the rhythm of her execution with a gasp. Then she begins the second movement of the litany.

You watch, without listening. The image takes over; you cut out the sound, switch off the lamentations. You are fascinated by Touma's attempt at a choreography, which ends in fiasco . . . Karagoz is resurrected, she is at one and the same time the presenter of the shadow-play and the grimacing shadow with fixed grin. She used to put on this performance once a year in the home you have left behind; most often to celebrate the anniversary of the father's death. 'My lost bulwark,' she would declaim, going on to invoke all the local saints, all the saints of the whole Islamic world, including Baghdad and Isfahan . . .

'Hajila, my daughter, you will bring misfortune on us all! On all your lineage, daughter of my withered loins, born of my cries of pain! We, poor lost sheep, who thought we were all fingers of one hand! . . . O, Sidi Abderahmane, ancestor of the ancestors of my dear departed mother, who is now happy in paradise! O, Sidi Yahia, from the mountain region of your father, who died a martyr!'

'My father did not die a martyr,' you interrupt her sharply; 'you know perfectly well independence had already been celebrated, and he was run over by a tractor on that farm.'

Touma stops clapping her hands and jerking spasmodically about. Only her gold ear-rings continue to toss beneath her red hair that escapes from her head-dress. She studies you as she resumes bitterly, 'Heartless daughter! You are ruined and you will be the ruin of us all!'

'I go out every day and I don't do anything wrong when I'm out,' you protest.

'When did you ever do anything wrong?' Touma snivels, her face bathed in tears as she stares severely at your hands, your dress.

She preached at you for an hour. She's nothing if not methodical, is your mother. And logical. You listened to her expounding the scheme she had banked on: the unexpected boon of a son-in-law who 'worked at the government' and who'd get them out of that slum where they never ought to have landed when, before the father's death in that accident, they'd lived in that comfortable villa in the city centre. Touma reminded you of all the subsequent events: the landslides that winter which made your neighbourhood dangerous; the evacuation of all the people living in your street; how the authorities had promised to rehouse them decently. The father may not have died a martyr, but still he had spent several years in prison, he must have had a card showing he'd been in the resistance. Well, when it was their turn to be rehoused, a neighbour who had more pull had got in before them. And they had ended up in this miserable hovel. And since then, the rest of the father's family – the ones who had their own *hammam*, all the others, the relatives who'd got rich recently – they wouldn't have anything to do with them any more. They were ashamed of them!

'The injustice of it! . . . D'you realize! What can a widow with two orphan daughters do these days, when we're supposed to be living in Islamic times? . . . This son-in-law, your master, isn't he the first sign that justice is waking up!'

You'd been married for six months. Touma was hoping for the announcement of a pregnancy which did not occur. She was going to speak to 'him'!

'Speak to . . .?'

'Yes! Ask him to intervene, to remind the government of their promise!' He'd got 'pull' too! . . . He could see they got the house they'd been promised, even after ten years!

'It's ten years Mma, ten years we've been forgotten! It's ages since anyone's even mentioned the people evacuated from the Dunes!'

'Your master could do something . . . I know he's also ashamed to see the wretched way we live; after all, we're his relatives now! . . . The other day he said himself he had to take a trip into the country!'

She smiled knowingly, opening her heart to you while she smoothed her hair and rearranged her satin head-dress.

'He was talking to your uncle and me, you weren't listening; he said, "I've got to go to visit some warehouses." For the service he's in charge of! . . .' (She repeated 'warehouses', like the refrain of a madrigal.)

'I heard him talking to his daughter,' you explain. 'I understand a little French now!'

'You always understood the language of the foreigners, when we lived in the Dunes, O Hajila, so aptly named, O liveliest of quails!'

He had been explaining, 'The state textile mills produce a lot of surplus; as the machines work non-stop, night and day, they have to increase the number of warehouses to store the surplus!'

'Warehouses to store . . .!' Touma muses enviously.

'They're not houses to live in!' you explain gently.

'All the same, it'll be the right moment to mention our problem to him! We're his relatives, we . . .'

She raises her arms; she begins to catch her breath – the prelude to another outburst.

'Hajila! you are ruined! You will be the ruin of us all! Is this my lot – to have brought you all to this misfortune! To have to go out to work, keeping house for that German, isn't mine a dog's life?'

'Shame mother! You've said yourself that you could stop if your son got work!'

'And Kenza, your young sister, does anyone have any idea where she will end up, poor girl! Do you ever think about her? If only we could get out of that slum, if only she could visit really nice people! . . . Oh, you bad girl! I'll stay here and keep you shut up at home and keep the Devil away! To think that in my old age I've still got to keep my eye on you, that the Prophet commands me to watch over my own flesh and blood, even in the "Man" 's own home! Oh, wretched girl! Why is it my fate to be so cursed!'

The doorbell interrupts this diatribe. The children follow each other in. They lower their voices, economical with the noise they make. Touma remains in the drawing-room. Nazim kisses you. In the kitchen he asks, 'Has she brought us any cakes?'

'Not this time, darling, but I'll make you some myself!'

Touma appears; she has calmed down.

'I'll make them straight away for my little prince, for the king's son, for my daughter Hajila's little page-boy!'

He looks down and smiles. Meriem has settled down with her bowl of steaming-hot chocolate. When Touma has turned her back she'll whisper her usual disrespectful remark to Nazim, about 'the witch with red fingers'.

You'd like to pacify the old lady. Since the two children came in, bringing something of the master's presence with them, you feel the need to comfort her, 'Mother, you can leave with your mind at rest!'

'How can my mind be at rest, when I'm the odd one out, the house without a roof, the barren tree?'

Nazim watches as Touma launches into another extempore performance; he doesn't understand unless there are rhymes and music. Touma puts on her veil in front of them, toning down her histrionics.

At the door, as you see her out, you are the repentant daughter (because the children are watching, because they catch the resemblance between the two of you, the same latent risk of ingrained docility); you bow your head, you take Touma's hands in your own cold hands. You humbly kiss her head, her forehead; you

47

feel her work-worn palms. You love her.

'Mma, go in peace and may Lla Aïcha, widow of the Beloved, of the Prophet, protect you and bring you solace!'

'Take good care of yourself, daughter! And take good care of us too, my precious!'

She whispers these last words as she stands at the open door. You wait at the lift. When Touma is out of sight you weep. You dab your cheeks, you dry your eyes. Then you go back in; you enter the sunny drawing-room, where the drama is nearing its dénouement.

'Never to go out again! Never again! How shall I bear it?'

You press your head against the wall. The window must be closed.

# 8

# THE OTHER

Every night, by imperceptible degrees, I increase my knowledge of 'the other' – trying out the hollow of his neck, testing the dependability of his shoulders, running a leisurely finger down his ribs, listening to his heartbeats, while keeping my eyes on his face; I slide my hand over his belly, down to his groin, tracing the familiar junction of his legs to his pelvis; feeling the shape of his skull, examining it with the eye of a scientist and the hands of an archaeologist. My caresses become the actions of a surveyor.

For long I used this means of possessing him, trying to extricate him from the hold his flesh and blood have on him.


The many sisters about whom I reminisce when we suddenly break into conversation in the semi-darkness. In fragile words I conjure up before him the pictures of four women. The eldest, with the face of a virtuous virgin, reached adolescence before him, although her passive good nature made her invariably take a back seat in the presence of the brother; the second, a year his junior, was formerly for him a source of affectionate concern – they think her to be sickly but I know she is his double in melancholia, this second sister, in whose lap I rested my head in those early days – we spent a year in the old house, weighing anchor there, attending the wedding of the third sister, a girl who, though of my own age, we sense is backward, but in respect of what, unless it be in finding some face to attach to love . . .

Why was I unaware of this third sister's sadness, so soon after the announcement of her engagement? Having received no wedding gifts ourselves, we showered presents on her to discover new ways of expressing our love. We hunted through all the jewellery stalls in the *medina* for an antique bracelet, probably Italian, with matching ear-rings, and in buying them, to re-create the pure joy of giving, as if to offer these jewels to each other, through the intermediary of this third sister who, when she was so adorned, seemed bedecked for sacrifice . . .

She ought to have had a wedding like ours – quiet to the point of austerity. But instead, the pale-faced bride with painted eyelids was escorted by a clamorous crowd; she suddenly turned her tear-filled eyes towards the two of us . . . The fourth sister appeared the day we first arrived, while I was still admiring the lemon tree and the ceramic tiling of the house – the last-born with the grace of a young she-goat, with her shy smile and that look of concentration that the man also adopts when he gets his fits of sulks and won't address a word to me. One summer evening, I run about barefoot, carrying my shoes in my hand; I call to the girl, while her brother saunters past. Would this fourth sister, with her love of childish games, do likewise? She looks up, troubled by the sound of our voices in the growing darkness.

The three of us spent the whole of that uneventful summer together, as if my beloved and I had agreed that we should escort the youngest in her dreamy passage through adolescence. So much so that, when we left, she felt we had abandoned her . . . A year later, she writes to tell us she is in love (she does not say with whom): a brief, pretentious note, leaving me with a confused sense of unease. I reread her words with apprehension: is she deluding herself, is she defying us, and why? Yet the man's only reaction to this admission by his sister is the calm assurance that everything will turn out well.

So, in the solitude of our bedroom, I talk to my husband at length about his sisters. I conjure up their presence. Night after night, I piece together the body of the man I love, with eyes that speak for me and groping hands that take the place of sight.

In the morning the man gets up. I move over to his side of the bed. However much I try to suppress the images of his sisters, I continue to be haunted by them. In my morning lethargy, I have to make an effort to drag myself out of this abyss of kinship.

How long has the mother's powerful image been standing there on the horizon of our dreams? She studies us as we lie open-eyed, hands alert, hair thrown back, in the whirlpool of our waking dreams, in the agitation of our bodies. The ghostly figure conjured up on the threshold finds consolation in what she sees.

Our dawns are moments of blissful calm; laughter comes more easily as the afternoons slip carelessly away and bedtime approaches. We wander through the endless empty rooms of the family home; the mother is waiting for us on the patio . . . When we go out, to the nearby orchards, to the crowded souks, to a suburban market, wherever we pause, I imagine I see her, an elderly lady with features emaciated by so much serenity!

As I drop off to sleep, I clasp my husband's hand, as if our doubles, ever conscious of each other's sleeping presence, were setting out on a nocturnal journey across devastated wastelands. On other nights, the mother's image steals between us, just as we wearily sink into oblivion.

Later, in another city, in a new country, we are gradually recovering the rhythm of our nights, the respiration of our days, when suddenly the mother's ghost returns and reminds us we are exiles. Am I the only one to be obsessed by this exile? I study her silhouette, enveloped in mauve tunics, the blur of her wax-pale face. What mortifications does she usher in?

This obsession with his origins is a sword thrust into the man, wounding him, startling him to his feet. For my part, I repudiate the ubiquitous matron. I repudiate her just as she is uniting us.


During the holidays spent in his childhood home, the three of us meet again at breakfast. 'What a pleasure,' the man exclaims, 'to sit and chat this morning! . . . To enjoy the summer together!'

'Maman . . .' I begin, as I pour the milk.

'I was up at four o'clock!' my mother-in-law interrupts. 'After my ablutions and early-morning prayers I went out into the garden! I picked this sprig of basil; it was so quiet, you could almost hear it growing!'

'It smells good!'

I turn towards my love. Under the mother's eyes, we offer each other milk, a handful of dates; but we don't sample the honey cakes. I eat heartily; I wish to share my pleasure in everything, even my most trivial observations:

'Listen! can you hear the water singing in the furrows?'

The old lady smiles; is she paying attention, or is she grieving? Her son and I slept late this morning; then we went out to greet her in the garden: with beaming faces, indolent gestures, we are ready to pour out our love for the whole world. The old nostalgia is gradually healed. The mother seems lost in a daydream; what lingering traces might her past yield up of a shared love, of one hour of fulfilment?

'Has the maid gone yet?'

I go into the drawing-room, where every surface sparkles, where our wedding photograph is on show, where ... I turn round suddenly, with a toss of my hair. She is gazing at her son with lacklustre eyes.

'I'm going out!' he declares.

'I'm coming with you!' I cry, and leave the cool drawing-room.

She reappears every night after that. Finding her way through the wildwood of our love-making. We observe a bedtime ritual: as drowsiness overcomes me, I cling close to the man, twining my legs around him. When I have fallen into my first deep sleep, I lie as I did as a girl – clasping the pillow to my chest, my head hanging over the side of the bed, and I plunge down into the rich turf of the night, from which we shall drift to the surface, just the two of us alone. He straightens my curled-up limbs, I anticipate his arms which haul me up like a fisherman; I try to curl up again and draw away ... His masculine strength encompasses me, holding me suspended.

One morning I found myself unexpectedly alone with my mother-in-law ... She has barely turned fifty and hasn't really aged much; her hair is jet-black but now she tints it; I had mixed the vegetable dye for her and spread the thick paste on her long, loose locks.

As I combed her hair, I declared, 'You are very beautiful! And I love you!'

She wiped away a tear. She was neither mollified nor gratified. I don't feel that she is easily hurt, but rather that she is difficult to understand, a mixture of affection and hardness. Later the same day, we have resumed our conversation, in the courtyard with its bright ceramic tiles which a woman is washing down with cans of water. Incredulously, I exclaim, 'You mean to say you breast-fed your son for . . . for three years?'

'Yes! It was wartime! There was a shortage of milk!' she reminisced.

'Doctors say . . .'

'It was wartime,' the mother interrupted and I, the daughter-in-law, was silenced.

The man's mother, enemy or rival, appears between the strata of our love-making. He has a nightmare just before daybreak: he is in the grip of what haunting memory? by what treachery is he torn? He thrashes about, he struggles. I wake up and try to calm him, stroking his brow, patiently, softly reassuring him.

He does not wake up; his open mouth utters a silent scream. What dream is gagging him? I have only one resource: I take off my nightgown and cling tightly to this body at war with itself. I mould my soft contours to his hard form, which is the prey to hallucinations, originating where? My prisoner tries to escape, I stubbornly hold on, he is in my grasp again, he roughly feels his way to me, sighs amid his caresses, is about to enter me when . . . A galloping black nightmare sends a fresh shudder through the sleeping features, the broad shoulders, the bare chest. His supine body becomes a thicket of fibres and nerves. His muscles contract, he feels for the gap, needing to find his way back to the faint reassuring murmur of the mother's womb.

I submit to him, with tears streaming down my face and terror in my heart. With perverse reluctancy I cling to his limbs and torso, stroke him gently, restoring his proud strength, soothe the sleeper whose phallus becomes erect. With gestures that perpetuate a timeless compassion, I drive away his nightmare. I present my face to the moonlight which pours in through our uncurtained window-panes.

Mingling tears and laughter in the blaze of a thousand nights with their dark corridors! We make our home again in the mother's lair, I, the wife, as ever sensitive to every signal, he, the son, whom I draw further and further away . . . Have I let him be reborn? or have I engulfed him? I cannot tell . . . But I have stolen him away from you, O Mother, to whom I defer, to whom I am bound, but whom I finally separate from the man I love.

# 9

# THE MAN

You have begun to go out again, Hajila. Every day your thin form moves through the city, borne along by the tempo of your unflagging enthusiasm.

As soon as you are up, you totter to the kitchen in the semi-darkness. The smell of toast wakens the children; you warm the milk for the man who arrives last and, in spite of your apparent care, it boils over on the stove. All four members of the household watch each other's movements in the white morning light – but you remain in the background: let the morning soon be over! Let it be the moment after lunch when you can get out! Till then you stay clear of the windows.

At midday the man returns. He is accompanied by the concierge's son, a tousle-headed lad of fourteen, carrying up the baskets of vegetables, fruit, the meat supply for several days, the freshly-slaughtered chicken. You finger the bunch of coriander and fresh mint. There is a covetous gleam in the boy's eyes – you don't know why. When he's put the baskets down he waits in the vestibule. Then he goes. The husband is in a hurry for his lunch; you linger at the sink, you make the coffee. He drinks standing up without a 'Thank you!' He leaves. You are alone.

Previously you used to lie down for a time in the children's room. The radio would spill out folk music – some days, Arab, some days, Berber. Recently you've not been switching it on. When you stay at home you prefer to let the sounds of the outside world reach you. There is so much for you to picture to yourself: not the traffic which you can hear rumbling and jolting past, but the people all around, women and children waiting to cross the road; you call up visions of the crowds jostling at the bus stops; you can hear the bus noisily turning the corner at the foot of your building, screeching to a halt

54

and creaking on its way again, soon after.

Now, you need more than these imaginings which have been your substitute for a siesta. You have resumed your afternoon expeditions. You return in the evening, noting that the sun has set behind the window of the drawing-room, which you had left open. You come back a little weary, but resonant with a store of sounds; you stand still, bending your head to catch the last echoes within you before they disappear; once again, your vision is hemmed in by walls.

Meriem has guessed something. One evening she circled round the table on which you'd left the crumpled veil lying like a bundle of rags. She didn't touch it; she just studied the woollen material; could she sniff secret odours? You appeared in the doorway, thinking, 'You will be spared this protective cloak, little girl!' You'd have liked to say it aloud . . . To pass on to her your own bitterness or hopes, to reach out your hand to her, but how can you fondle the daughter of the woman who is a stranger to you?

She stared at you suspiciously. You rolled the rag up into a ball (repeating bitterly to yourself, 'Yes, this rag!'); Meriem resumed her idling round the table, dragging one arm stiffly over its surface. In the street below a beggar struck up a plaintive chant.

In spite of the late hour, you asked Nazim to take him down a coin. A moment later he's back, followed by his father. Who reprimands you. You don't reply. The beggar is still singing: it suddenly seems very hot.

You find your voice at last: 'A stranger's blessing can protect us all!'

The man paused behind you. Without turning round you could sense his astonishment; you would have liked to add 'O Master, I do more than that; you'll find out one day!' These words roll around inside you.

He leaves you; during this tense exchange, Nazim has not moved. Now he rubs against your skirt, showing you his sore ears. 'He pinched them till they bled!' he complains with a tremble in his voice.

'My darling, my precious heart! . . . One day you'll be a big boy and . . .'

You cannot continue. You stroke his head. He smiles up at you. Then he starts to lay the table.

In the other bedroom, at the end of the passage, the man is carrying on a conversation with the little girl. You catch Meriem's slightly nasal voice. Without curiosity.

'Meriem,' Nazim begins.

'Your father is hearing Meriem recite her lesson. What about you?'

'No, she's not going over her lesson.'

After a moment's silence, he resumes, 'She's telling him secrets!'

'And where would she find secrets, my little prince?'

'Everywhere, Mma . . . Every time we come home from school, Meriem always says, "I can guess everything that's hidden! I'm a magician, I am!" '

'Hush! You'd better be doing some work!'

'Yes, Mma, I'm trying!'

You start thinking of Touma and her hysterical outbursts, of all those burlesque portrayals of suffering throughout the long years of wretched poverty.

The three others have finished their dinner. You remain alone in the kitchen, moving utensils about, turning on the tap, rinsing your soapy hands. You've finished the washing-up; the water is still running in the sink, but you sit down on the tiled floor, your legs bent, your head resting on one knee. The sighing respiration of the night is all around you. Suddenly a barb of anxiety stabs you: suppose another day never dawned, suppose you were never to go out again, suppose you were never able to walk about in the sunlight again, suppose . . .

You hear steps in the passage. You get up, your heart beating fast. Did you fall asleep on the floor, or was it a nightmare? You are haunted by the echo of your mother's wails: 'You will be ruined, you will be the ruin of us all, daughter of my shrivelled womb!'

You plunge your trembling hands into the soap-suds. The man is standing there, wearing only his pyjama trousers, blinking in the harsh light.

'Hurry up with the washing-up! . . . Come to bed!'

'The children . . .' you murmur.

'The children have been asleep for ages! I've put their light out! Come!'

His deep voice has a different tone. He seems to have grown in size. You notice how hairy his chest is. (You had just commented to yourself at dinner, 'What enormous fingers he's got! . . . Goodness, he's got hairs on his knuckles!') Since you've been going out every day, you've started to notice separate details of other people's forms. Before this, the man moved about before you in a sort of blurred halo.

He has gone back to the bedroom. He is barefoot. Had he seen you crouching down on the floor? You begin to wish you were back in the little yard, where at this very moment your sister must be washing the dishes and saucepans in the water she'd fetched in a petrol-can from the communal tap.

'Kenza is living in poverty, while I'm becoming a doll kept in luxury!'

Your tears flow in a delayed reaction – the continuous drama of your childhood catches up with you in this new setting. You weep for your family's poverty, for the bad luck that has dogged you all since the father's death, since you were a little girl . . . You dry your hands, your eyes, your cheeks. The voice at the end of the corridor calls your name twice: is it really your name? – 'Hajila! Hajila!' Twice.

You switch out the light in the kitchen; you enter the bedroom; you walk over to the bed which is too high.

'Come!' the man whispers. The light from a lamp placed low down is reflected in his eyes.

You fumble with your collar; you start to unbutton your blouse. He has got out of bed, he grabs you by the shoulders; the patch of light from the lamp seems to diminish his action, while casting long shadows into the four corners of the room, as in a dream. You clench your teeth.

Rape! Is this rape? People assert that he is your husband, your mother always refers to 'your master, your lord' . . . He has forced you down on to the bed, you try to fight him off, finding unsuspected sources of strength. You are crushed beneath his chest. You try to wriggle free from under the weight, you stiffen your arms convulsively against your sides, bracing yourself as he clasps you to him. The man's arms tighten around you, then relax their grip, you bend your legs, not daring to kick, not trying to escape. A battle fought out on a mattress in a tangle of crumpled sheets . . . The man has switched out the lamp, taking advantage of a temporary let-up, a brief breathing space. You were already

57

closing your eyes. The climax is near, you resume your resistance.

The man is breathing hard against your neck; he seems to be laughing, half surprised: 'It's good! . . . You don't want it, but it's good!'

He nibbles the lobe of your ear, the base of your neck; he drags you up towards him, pulls your head back. The moment is approaching when you will have to go under. Closing yourself off, shutting eyes, ears, the depths of your heart. Letting yourself sink!

'Don't be afraid, little one!' He utters incomprehensible words.

Must you surrender? No! Think of the streets, they stretch out within you, bathed in the sunshine that has dissolved the storm clouds; the walls open; trees and hedges glide past. You can see the space out of doors through which you sail each day. When the man's penis ruptures you, with one rapid sword-thrust, you scream out in the silence, breaking your own silence, 'No! . . . No!' You struggle against him, he castigates you, you try to return to the surface. 'Just relax!' the voice murmurs, near your temple. You are being torn apart; the procession of streets unwinds within you, shadowy passers-by turn back and stare at you, steady streams of unknown people with bulging eyes.

The penis is still in place, the burning pain spreads, the darkness blots out all your defensive visions. You are conscious only of this squelching sound. The man has withdrawn, your legs hang limply; in the sudden spurt of light from the lamp, you survey with tear-drenched eyes the blood spreading over the sheets, over the bare mattress . . . the man has disappeared into the bathroom. When he returns he tosses you a towel; it lies over your blood-stained legs.

'He can see my legs! He can see my blood! He has paid for this right! . . .'

He has changed into clean pyjamas. He lies down again, with a cigarette. You wouldn't straighten the sheets, you haven't remade the bed, you've gone to lie down on the floor, on your usual mattress. You curl up. 'He' lies on his high bed with the light still on; he seems to want to talk, you don't listen, he's been your master for six months now, or possibly seven, you've lost count. It's done now: outside is another country. Your blood smells; you refuse to wash. Let the man sleep, while you listen to his breath whistling! He called you once or twice in the dark: 'Come! . . . Come and sleep

58

here!' You pretended not to hear.

At dawn, before the first light of day could catch you unawares, you washed your legs, stomach, pubic region in boiling-hot water; then your neck, arms, face. You've respected the ritual of ablutions, although you are barred from all prayers.

Back in your former home, Touma used to like to squat down in the little yard; she would tuck her gaudy *saroual* up above her knees with sighs of relief. Most often it was siesta time. You would hurry to join her when you were little, Hajila, and even as an adolescent. You would listen to your mother's story emerge from her flood of murmurs: overlapping reminiscences, events recalled in fits and starts, according to the vagaries of memory, while the sun shone. through the vine leaves on to the narrator's forehead, eyes . . . The same story, so often repeated, at the same time, in the same dazzling sunlight, then the words dry up. And Touma would find nothing more to say for weeks on end.

She was married when she was twelve. The husband had first gone to work in the capital, then he had crossed the Mediterranean. Touma conjures up the olive groves and lentisk trees of the grandfather's home, where she had given birth to her first child: three years after her marriage, she was spending all her time weeding and hoeing between the trees, helping her mother-in-law with the olive-picking. 'I was so strong!' Touma recalls. 'But my mother-in-law let me off some of the work when she saw I was pregnant!'

The old peasant folk looked forward to the child's birth, an heir for their heir.

'I gave birth to you!' the mother said.

She plunges once more into her memories; her dull eyes linger on you, Hajila, as you squat down in the yard listening.

'The old people didn't want to let their son know! A daughter! What good is that! Your father returned when you were eight months old. He used to love to lift you up in the sun with a laugh. The old lady, the Lord preserve us, was jealous when she saw how happy he was with the two of us, when you were tiny! When I was pregnant for the second time, and the man had gone away again, I did all the work: weeding, hoeing. I even climbed the olive trees to shake the branches; afterwards I was completely done in: I couldn't sleep at night for backache! And it was another girl!'

Kenza stifled a mischievous laugh; she knew what was coming next. The father returned from France and left again; every day the old lady found some new quarrel to pick with Touma, and the children never had enough to eat. The mother worried about you, the eldest, and got up in the night to steal olive oil out of the jar to keep you quiet when you moaned with colic from excruciating diarrhoea. The old grandmother would pause in her pot-making to grumble, 'Let the Lord take her back! . . . If it's written that her destiny is to be cut short! . . . What do we want with yellow-faced females!'

Touma became pregnant for a third time; the child was still-born, 'because of all the work' – in the fields as well as in the house, which all devolved on her. The old grandmother was now half-blind and never left her mattress. The grandfather didn't sell any more pottery. The olive crop was less and less adequate. The father came back for the summer and decided to stay. The whole family moved to the capital, to a rented room in the old quarter; distant cousins who'd settled in the city helped them. But the troubles of the war of independence began. Eventually a sickly boy, Nasser, was born; shortly afterwards the legionnaires came to arrest the father who was accused of briefly harbouring a 'terrorist'. For several days the whole area was cordoned off; the little girls occasionally ventured as far as the doorway, where they breathed the silence of collective fear . . .


Hajila, you listened to the story of your past unfold: the time spent on the Kasbah with your mother's cousins; the endless anxiety, the impatience as the end of the war was in sight. The frenzy that swept through the city when independence was declared, the tidal wave of joy, ready to spill over, engulfing everyone. Two girls, plunged in daydreams, regardless of the intoxication all around, lost in contemplation of the whitewashed walls, the ancient terraces and always, and especially, that distant view of the sea. The whole landscape, with its splashes of violent colours, crackled with an explosion of joy mixed with tears!

The father was released from the Barberousse prison; his old

parents had died meantime. Touma had become hardened by all
the work she had had to undertake in order to survive, in addition to
her daily visits to the prison. Now she moved with all her family to a
villa requisitioned in the Dunes district. At last she could reign
supreme over her own kingdom! But the French people, departing
in a hurry, had left all their furniture which seemed to be expecting
their return; so Touma got rid of all the ornaments, books,
sculptures (there was a variety of plaster statues, 'their idols!' she
grumbled) to the local second-hand dealer. In exchange he gave her
a number of mattresses; she set the girls to work making
bed-covers, embroidering cushions, eager for a salon like they have
in Fez or Tlemcen, to entertain the neighbours who never came to
visit!

The father found work – repairing agricultural implements on a
farm in the nearby Sahel. He soon became a member of the
'committee of management'; he returned home late every evening,
the family saw hardly anything of him. Even on his weekly days off,
he went to endless meetings. He became more taciturn than ever;
his daughters scarcely even caught a glimpse of him when he got up
first thing in the morning. Sometimes Hajila, still only half-awake,
would hear the vague murmur of her parents carrying on
discussions at dawn: she would strain her ears to make out her
father's voice which seemed to punctuate Touma's diatribes. One
day she clearly heard her mother listing all her past and present
expenses. Every now and again the father would repeat, 'As you
wish, woman! . . . as you wish, woman!' His voice was warm, but its
intonation seemed weary, submissive. This auditive memory
remained embedded in Hajila's mind like a splinter.

For the father . . . Alas! the accident: a day beginning like any
other day, but by nightfall ending in women's lamentations.
Howling everywhere: in the street (Touma had rushed out without
her veil, strangers brought her back screaming, her face already
lacerated), inside the house too. Hajila and Kenza stood frozen
against the wall while women and still more women, unknown
women, female relatives, all droned and groaned, red-eyed, with
crumpled veils, mingling their scents, all crowding round Touma
who lay in a cataleptic fit, apparently unconscious . . . The long
wake of misfortune: it was as if the visitors had been waiting for this.
Hajila tried to find her father, her father's body, the body they had

buried . . . Like a gaping wound, a fatal absence in the midst of all those veils, those tunics, those head-dresses in disarray from which wisps of red hair escaped over foreheads flushed with heat. Hajila ran from the house, fleeing from that villa in the Dunes. Does it still exist? The father was buried far away, in his native village; neither of the girls went to the funeral. Only Touma and little Nasser.

'Mother, married at the age of twelve!' you repeat to yourself this morning as you prepare the breakfast, tight-lipped. 'Still a child! Her child's blood! . . . Am I like her this morning, although I am twenty-four? I shall never know, she will never tell . . .' The village women would have brandished the pathetic bridal nightgown, the match-maker would have danced with the blooded cloth, her mouth gaping wide to reveal the gleam of her gold teeth!

After the father's death, Touma had had to sell her jewellery . . .

When you've given the children their breakfast, Hajila, you go to bathe again. You lock the bathroom door. The steam from the hot water mists over the pink tiled walls.

The man tries the lock. He bangs unceremoniously on the door. You open it and stand rigidly facing him. 'I've a right to the Turkish baths!' you declare. 'I shall go to the Turkish baths!'

'I shall go to the local Turkish baths!' you repeat louder, as you let him in.

'I'll fetch your mother tomorrow, she can accompany you!' he decides.

He speaks in his usual voice, quiet and composed.

'No! I want my sister; I want Kenza!' you retort. (Your voice is scathing.) 'My mother . . . how can I tell her? Now! . . .'

You look up, you are standing quite close to him. You stare at him defiantly. You let a brief flash of derision appear; let him realize that, if he refuses, you'll make no bones about declaring, 'You were impotent! You poor masculine specimen!'

You push past him.

This morning, the day after the rape, you are no longer afraid of him. You only have to remember the times you stroll at liberty through the sunlit spaces of the town, with no stench between your legs.

The door slams. You return to the bathroom, full of confidence in yourself.

Every night, for nearly a week, you suffer. 'Now that he's no longer impotent, will every night be a trial for me?' you wonder, appalled in the face of this sea of noxious emanations. 'Is this what coitus really is for every woman? this physical pain?' Has no woman ever rebelled? Do the other forms of slavery not suffice? The endless daily round of toil? The endless succession of childbearing? . . . They gave you to understand, didn't they, that a woman's life began like a festival? The celebrations were brief, to be sure, and followed by the unavoidable acceptance of a lifetime's heartache! . . . But when does the rejoicing start? When does a woman enjoy even one day of ecstasy?

At the family weddings you attended, you always avoided the groups of girls who crowded excitedly round a few newly-weds on the night of the new bride's deflowering. You kept your distance, imagining these young wives describing their thrills, their transports perhaps, to the expectant virgins, with shining eyes and flushed cheeks; it was as if the wreaths of jasmin on their heads, the garlands round their necks would never fade till they came close to this sensual experience. You avoided these groups and their mutual confessions; you are sorry now: you were embarrassed, it's true, by your shabby dress which had seen better days, and your meagre jewellery. You resented the fact that your cousins never let you forget your home in the shantytown, from where you'd set out that morning, with your mother and sister to bring your wedding gifts! You were the ones who'd come down in the world . . . 'How will my daughters ever be accepted in these "nice" homes?' Touma would moan . . . The other girls talked about the man, about the first night, about other nights; they gave minute descriptions of the fondlings, caresses, exchanges of endearments ('what endearments?' you wonder cynically in your kitchen). Sometimes they added that 'they' even used French words picked up in the brothel!

Yes, these women were lying, they were all lying, in spite of the scent of jasmin flowers round their foreheads, or the match-maker's obscene gestures as she danced around with the nuptial night-gown's evidence of the rape! Why? The myth was perpetuated on the patios. No woman had dared to admit, 'There is a stench of blood between your legs. Every night this searing burrows deeper into you, you clench your teeth for minutes on end, waiting for the male to finish puffing and panting above your head!' Not one of

63

these women revealed that, the following morning, your only defence is defiance! You take your time washing yourself, oh so slowly! you show your hostility by the way you stand against a door. And the man goes away.

'For I shall go out again,' you say to yourself, a week later. A week of detention. Kenza let your husband know that the visit to the Turkish baths would have to be put off for a week. Unclean, stricken, washing yourself every morning in the pink-tiled bathroom, you beat against the walls . . .

One night, the sixth, you refused to take your place on the high mahogany bed. 'I want the *hammam* first!'

He didn't reply. You slept soundly, heavily, as if in a drunken stupor. You woke later than usual, feeling refreshed. In your new gentle mood, you lavish infinite attentions on the children. Days of insecurity. Poor innocents, whose fault is that?

Kenza arrived unexpectedly at lunchtime, accompanied by your brother Nasser – at fifteen he'd just started his apprenticeship as a mechanic. She sat down in the drawing-room. She calmly took off her veil. When Nasser and the man had left, you embraced her again; and you burst into tears. She dried your cheeks, asking no questions. During your shared adolescence, she was always the one to make the decisions.

'We'll go to the baths presently! Don't cry, dear Hajila!'

'I'm unclean! What would I have done if you hadn't come today! I'm . . .'

And you were about to repeat nervously, 'I'm . . .'

'May the Prophet be my witness, we really couldn't manage! Mother had to go out every morning, the German needed her, and he's just paid her three months' wages!'

You're no longer listening. You cannot wait to get to the bath-house, to be among all those worn-out bodies, finding relief in the soothing atmosphere. If you are really never to go out again, at least to be able to open up one's eyes, breasts, armpits! To lie, resting one's back on the scorching marble slab, wet hair spread loosely, belly, genitals, legs liberated, hollowing out a cave where one can commune with oneself at last, that real self whom no one knows.

# 10

# WORDS

Our words throw light on neither pain nor joy; they are snares. Their tintinnabulation wells from springs of passion. The half-darkness inveigles them into our bed, just as our transports approach flash point.
The window overlooks the shadowy garden. The lamp has been switched off. Still heavy with sleep, I struggle back to consciousness. I am aware of the muttered sounds emerging from the sleeper's lips and scattering round the room like fragments of a shattered nut.
'Oh! . . .' There follows a passionate outpouring of incomprehensible names.
I open my eyes in the darkness in an effort to grasp the sounds and their meaning. I am ensnared in their toils. I struggle to free myself. The icy tentacles of my lover's words wrap around me, while our voices hang in the air.
I clutch at the man's shoulders. In his sleep he spills out a flood of words, needle-sharp. My last dreams before dawn are cross-hatched by this delirium; I catch sleep-walking fragments. An expression of harsh desire awaits me, planted in the golden light of a new dawn.

As twilight falls the next evening, we find ourselves in a maze of narrow streets that all end in blind alleys, against a horizon of glowing embers. Back in our room, the window-pane watches our embraces. The growing darkness creeps between us. We go out.
We return from these flights to take refuge in the waiting bed. Our simplest actions are an effort; our throats are constricted with craving; our eyes grow heavy, blinded by the turbulence of surrounding objects.

We are haunted by images which won't leave us in peace – the booty brought back from our wanderings. They try to escape through every outlet of the body: twitching eyes, open hands, the mutterings of dry lips. Our muscles are heavy with fatigue.

Half-asleep, the man stretches out to settle my head in the hollow of his shoulder; pulls my thigh against his side. And begins to speak.

He gives vent to a tremolo of words that fall on my ears as empty shapes. Describing in advance movements, postures, figures the body will adopt; announcing the way to break down any reserve, precipitate expectation . . . Muscles grow sluggish, a leg or joint is slow to react, as if to express the denial of the flesh . . . Words precede the encounter, anticipate resistance. Imperceptible approach to tacit consent.

I let the sounds enclose me; my lover's voice breaches the barriers of the night. Protected from any regrets, I abandon myself without reserve, in a solemn expenditure of sensuality. Gradually sleep closes over us.


At times each partner gropes towards the other, and draws away again after a mutual recognition, actions repeated many times, over many nights, without a word spoken. Rasping agony of the tongue incapable of communication. Heart spilling over with love.

Once more, sudden surrender, steep escarpments of the approach, momentum renewed, then subsiding. Suddenly, unpredictably, I resist. At the height of the nocturnal struggle I decide to put up the barricades. While my arms are already flung open in welcome, I anticipate the intrusion, I provoke it, then in a sudden turnabout, I am defiant. I thrash about, biting and scratching. My husband is perplexed by this violence.

Nights of obscure confrontations. 'Oh, what a dark tunnel!' I sigh. If the light were dimmed, I could unburden myself. It is the man's turn to be stubborn. He insists on explanations. I would only have to find a few words, express my fears by the tone of my voice; we would enjoy a respite. My regrets become sharper: 'What a dark tunnel I have led us into!'

I imagine myself pleading. I undress. The man thinks to himself, before the nightly ritual of our love-making, 'Her gestures have not the soft curves of surrender, nor smooth-flowing indolence that is the prologue to passion, but her body is all angles, arms hesitate, in an economy of effort.'

I pull my blouse over my head, in the usual way. I throw off garments of silk or flannel; my elbows trace alternating arabesques in front of lace-covered breasts, my hands slide down to my hips and the skirt slips off, over my knees – all this time I keep my eyes lowered, my expression subdued, deliberately reticent.

The man remains a spectator. When I come and bury my head in the hollow of his shoulder, he switches off the light, happy that our ritual is resumed. In the depths of the night, a word uttered in a half dream by one or other of us breaks through the barrier. I wake up, set free, I hear myself murmur, 'I've found you again ! . . . It seems so long since . . .'

I switch on the lamp again, studying the dear face: midnight reconciliation. I shower kisses on the husband's forehead, eyelids, wrists . . . with face bathed in tears, I cannot halt the flow of words: wild words from a wild sister, begging for love, for forgiveness . . . it is all my fault . . . We embrace, the man lets himself be swayed by my tone of supplication.

The passage from arousal to pleasure follows a meandering course: I continue the assurances of my love, I deny him my lips so that I can go on talking, weaving a tangle of passionate words. At last my lips find no more words, only hissed, muted, babbled accompaniment of orgasm . . . The voice tails away, the body is cast up on familiar shores, I dwell once more in a world of silence coloured by emotion.

Once more the couple exchanges trivial conversation; a day when we are walking in the rain. Uncertain words. Returning at nightfall to resume our mutual quest. Suddenly I shut myself off; the man, at a loss in the face of my unexpected inflexibility, stops short and is silenced. The whole of the following day will be submerged in a flood of unpredictable words. Trivial, meaningless conversations.

Words of shot-silk, you float in the air like fairy-lights at a fair, oranges glowing among snow-covered foliage. He called me, it was midnight or four in the morning, just before daybreak; through the open window a dappled sky turns ashen, then milk-white. I wake up completely, asking, 'What did you say?'

Sometimes I insist, I'm afraid of forgetting the word, for he called me by the name of some graceful creature of the savannah, that he was probably dreaming of, while still at my side. Sometimes he names some rare fruit, as if he were offering me the word itself, or some common or garden plant that had taken root in his dreams. If we unwind our legs, link arms again, would I then, in my turn, succeed in drawing him into the heart of my nocturnal imagery? All the gentle words welling up in his throat draw us close against each other. We crumble these words as we simultaneously crumple the sheets that enfold us each night.

And the night is set ablaze again in this landslide of words.

# 11

# THE RETURN

Hajila, you did not know that I had returned to this city after so many years away. At eighteen, a rebellious adolescent, I used to go to secret meetings with my lover, saying to myself, 'If father finds out, I shall kill myself!' Eventually we got formally engaged; nevertheless, the day before the ceremony, I did try to kill myself. In an uncontrollable fit of madness.

I was returning to the scenes of my juvenile defiance. My daughter had written to me: 'Maman, I don't want . . . to stay with them!'

I waited for her father in the street, near his car.

'You promised, if she couldn't get used to . . .'.

'But you insist on living abroad! You know the law wouldn't let you have custody!'

He was sounding me out.

'Why shouldn't I come back here for good? Looking after my daughter would be sufficient reason, wouldn't it!'

He looked at me suspiciously, an ugly expression on his face.

'In a month's time, I'll have made the necessary arrangements,' I said. 'I shall get a job in my home town.'

'The thing is . . . I want to see my daughter, too!'

To put an end to the argument, I reminded him of our contract: that we should not live in the same town as each other, even though separated. I then turned my back on him.

The next day I was far too busy, visiting every female member of my extended family: aunts, cousins, most of them showing signs of age, like best clothes, kept for special occasions in a cupboard, with moth-balls, and from time to time taken out to air, all creased and crumpled. These women were withering prematurely, from being permanently shut up indoors.

I went to meet Meriem every day when she came out of school; she told me in her determined little voice, 'My father's new wife is beginning to get a big tummy, Maman!'

Her brother arrived from the adjoining school. I saw them across the road. I hummed to myself, as I departed. Periods when life stretches out in front of one again, when the river runs smoothly onwards.

So, you discover you are pregnant, Hajila! Back in the shantytown, Touma welcomes the news with shrill cries of joy; you watch her throat vibrate in triumphant ululations. What triumph? what defeat? . . . 'Is it possible that I shall never go out again?' you think.

Imperceptibly, we are approaching the climax of the drama.


I am glad of the premonition that caused me to take my daughter away, to spare her the sight of the shouting, the blows, the incredible sexual stupidity . . . As it turned out, after two or three meetings in the lawyer's office (he confirmed my rights), the father gave in. When Meriem came out of school, she took my hand, never to leave me again; her suitcase had been sent to me the day before.

'You'll soon be going to a new school! We're going to live in the town where I grew up. I shall be working there now!'

We've started a new life: Meriem, who is so frail, although she is six already, sleeps in my bed every night. Every morning, she dawdles in the bathroom, just like me.

When I get a job in an infants' school (I shall start teaching the mother tongue again), I shall only have to open the window of the classroom during singing lessons to be able to hear the chorus of children from the next classroom. If I concentrate hard, I shall be able to distinguish the voice of my only child.

At playtime, we shall be able to say hallo to each other, discreetly screwing up our eyes, pretending we're wearing masks; we shall continue our little conspiracy on our way home, until night-time unites us again. 'It's all over,' I say to myself, as I wander through the Roman ruins. 'What does it matter to me if, by some misfortune, I should find myself caught up in some taboo, if I should be wrapped around once more by the *haïk* of tradition? I hold my daughter's hand to drag her into the sunlight; I shall prevent her

from being swallowed up!'
In the tumult of the capital, your story continues, O my sister.


The man had started drinking again; you would come upon him unawares, careless of his appearance. So it was now his turn to drop the veil, with the difference that you did so in the open air, while he remained in camera, for you have discovered, each time you make your escape, that all men have a secret hiding-place in which they skulk! You imagined 'outdoors' to be full of males, who could stroll about at their own sweet will . . . But you hadn't understood: when men go out, it is to expose our hurts, the sufferings that they have inflicted on us for generations, that we carry like stigmata – terrible fathers, taciturn brothers who imprison themselves with us, when they condemn women's bodies to be concealed!

The man now brought back bottles of beer together with the baskets of provisions, except that the basketsful lasted two or three days; while the supply of beer, like the bread, was renewed daily. Always the same brand of beer, from the nationalized breweries. He carried them in himself, storing them in a compartment of the fridge that the children couldn't reach.

When they were asleep, he didn't settle down in the mahogany bed any more, with a book and the occasional availability of your body. No. He came back to the kitchen. The first time, he took out a coloured glass that you'd never seen before. He asked you to get the bottles out of the fridge.

'You open one first!' Then he added, 'You can drink with me, if you like!'

You stood with your arms dangling at your side and shook your head. Not contemptuously; you can't stand the smell. You left him there in that white-tiled room that, every evening, becomes his prison. And you go off to sleep, alone at last, lying flat on the floor.

He wanders about the flat, walks up and down the passage, opens doors; once you heard him vomiting in the lavatory. Nazim tosses in his sleep, he calls you softly; you don't get up. 'Damn the man!' you sigh. He inspires you with neither pity nor fear.

In the morning you thought that he must be suffering from some strange illness. The disgusting noise in the lavatory, the night before, seemed like a symptom of disease.

71

The days seem to slip by ... Since that time, at the Turkish baths, when you had to admit to your sister, 'If now, for the second month I can't purify myself, then, yes, I must be pregnant!'

'Thanks be to the Prophet!' Kenza muttered (the first time at the baths, in spite of the soothing heat, you hadn't managed to confess to the rape). 'Mother will be pleased ... and relieved! You realize, don't you, what our old women are like! They don't consider that you're protected by a man, unless you're carrying his child!'

'Who will that one be able to protect?' you retort, adding bitterly, 'Every evening, in his own home, he drinks!'

'May the Lord preserve us all, Hajila dear!' Kenza sighs sadly.

By the time you leave the baths, flushed beneath your drapery, she has recovered her good humour. Trotting along, bundled up in your woollen veils, you could almost imagine yourselves back in that comfortable home in the Dunes. You made fritters for tea; when the children returned from school, they admired your healthy colour, the lacy pattern of henna outlining the palms of your hands and the sheen of your long hair.

'What an affectionate nature this boy has!'

'I think the girl's going to live with her mother!' you observe.

'So, he wasn't a widower; he was divorced! Was the mother really a foreigner? Did each of the children have a different mother?'

'How do I know?' you reply.


From that day you accept the fact that you are pregnant; you carry a future within you; for whom? For the drunkard who vomits every night at the end of the passage? For yourself? You couldn't care less; you have resumed your escapes. Since the fridge has been stocked up with beer, you can sleep; you no longer need to annihilate the misery you felt in the beginning, and the numbness that ensued. Alone, on your mattress, you spend your nights undisturbed.

It is daybreak. You rapidly perform all your domestic duties. In the afternoon, once you are out of the house, you discover new façades, new faces. Noises enfold you; from time to time the distant murmur hangs suspended in a tree, like a pearl, the goldfinch pierces the blue air with its shrill note ... You expose your skin to the sun; you rejoice uninhibitedly in the gusts of wind that sometimes sweep the surface of the roadway. You always walk without a veil.

For the second month again, you had no need to purify yourself; you are carrying a life, what life, life is all around you, out of doors, a quivering mosaic of dreams. Without a veil! How can one carry a child for endless months? 'Are there any women moving around outside who are heavy with child?' you wonder. 'Have I seen any pregnant women, women who are pregnant and go out unveiled? Foreign women who are going to the doctor's and who will have their babies in a nursing home!'

You recall that neighbour in the shantytown who, with every pregnancy, packed her wicker basket and insisted on her husband (an unskilled worker in a government factory) taking her back to her tribe on the high plateaux, near the western border. She couldn't imagine giving birth anywhere except among the women of her own flesh and blood.

'To receive their blessing!' she explained, adding, with a sort of naïve vanity, as she had been delivered of seven children in the same way, 'Otherwise, where would I find the strength to bear all that pain, to scream for hours on end, and not kill myself?'

But she always conceded somewhat ambiguously, 'Eventually, you get to like that damned pain of childbirth! You begin to pour blessings on yourself . . .'

You're not worried for the moment about the birth. You know that the man will deposit you in a nursing home, among strange nurses and doctors, that he'll come to see you in the same way, interested in the sex of the infant. He'll bring your mother, subdued for once, to visit you, and what then? No, it's not the pain of giving birth in an ice-cold universe which torments you. It's the present waiting period, this heaviness which you find hard to accept: how will you possibly be able to move around out of doors without being seen? How can you escape notice with this swollen belly? Will this protuberance take on your identity, fend the air for you to pass, prevent your being an observer whose appetite is never satisfied?

Will you never be alone again when you walk? Will you lose your light step? Is there any fleeting hope, hope of . . .? You realize you are approaching a mystery, which will dissolve as soon as it is touched.

'Do you suppose I could get rid of it?' you whisper in Kenza's ear, as she embraces you the following day, when you go to visit your family.

'The foetus?' she nearly screams in a panic. 'Get Satan behind you, Hajila!'

She avoids you, thinking probably of their hopes for a better life. Your husband, during the last month, has listened several times to the mother's request; she's reeled off once more the detailed chronological account of their eviction, just as she had done the day of the formal marriage proposal – which seems a hundred years ago! Her son-in-law promised, 'I've made out an application. There's a waiting-list for subsidized housing, several months at least! But one of the officials comes from my native region.'

'My son!' wept Touma, planting a kiss on the man's shoulder. She clung on to him, under your eyes.

'I'll wait till you've moved,' you promised Kenza. 'I'll let you all get settled into the promised "four-roomed house". Then, come what may, I'll get rid of the foetus!'

'Don't expect me to help you!' Kenza protests. 'Don't let mother hear you, please!' she adds querulously. 'She feels that this is something that concerns her personally!'

That same evening, while washing the dishes in the sink, you mused, 'At last Kenza will live in a house with running water . . .' You envy her. 'She'll have water, but no man in her bed, the lucky girl!'

The following night, you watch your husband get steadily more drunk. You hear the noise of the shutters; a moment before, you've been alerted by the sound of broken glass. You rush into the kitchen where all the lights are on; you scream with fright . . .

The man is hanging over the balcony. You run and tug at him, bruising yourself against his shoulders as you shake him against the frame of the french window; in this prelude to the main action you hear my name for the first time as he mutters, over and over again, wild-eyed, 'Isma! . . . Isma!'

You recoil at this name, my name. Then you push the drunkard, like a beast of burden, out into the passage, back to the bedroom. He collapses on to your mattress on the floor. He falls asleep, breathing heavily. You leave the room and go to pick up the pieces of the broken window-pane; you hide the empty bottles as he has been used to doing every evening. Eventually you slip into bed with

Nazim who has been calling you in the dark; you press his head against your breast. You try to pacify him as he is crying spasmodically.

Finally, he admits, 'You know, Mma, my sister Meriem's leaving tomorrow, she's going to live with her own mother?'

You'd seen her suitcase being taken away that very morning; you hadn't asked any questions.

'My mother's French,' he tells you; 'she left me with her parents a long time ago. I've never seen her again! Then I went to live with my father and his wife, Meriem's mother, a few months before we came here . . . We all came back here together, except for the lady!'

'I'm your mother, I'm Hajila, your mother!' you exclaim, surprised at your own exuberance. You hold him in your arms, soothing him tirelessly, until he falls asleep. Lying open-eyed in the darkness, you dream of wandering with the child, through the moonlit streets.

While, I, Isma, am preparing to leave the city for good, why did I not foresee the tragedy? Why am I condemned to provoking separation and discord? Why, since I've returned to the scenes of my adolescence, can I not be a healer of wounds?

# 12

# PATIOS

Now that I have reached this point in my story, I have no choice but to merge my life with that of another woman. Does the body of every male serve to indicate the crossroads towards which we women spin, blindfold, out of control, holding out our hands towards each other?

Patios of my childhood! Settings for the daily assembly, you were at the heart of all the domestic conspiracies which continue to haunt me. Women seated there, sometimes several wives of one man, or grouped in the shadow of the same master – father, elder brother, both earning more respect than a husband, who might be temporary. For the most part, these women were related by marriage – near or distant relatives – but all warmed by the affection they felt for a common ancestor.

I can remember a Moorish house, the oldest and largest in the area where I was born. Arcades of twisted marble columns, galleries whose ceramic tiles of copper-colour, pale blues and faint greens retained their harmony in spite of age: two storeys rose up around the courtyard, where I was fascinated by the fountain when I came every afternoon in summer to visit an aunt.

Three different branches of the family lived there, each one on a different level; the patriarch, a leading citizen of former times, had had three wives in succession, the last one being my grandmother who had barely reached puberty when she came there as a bride. She was the same age as some of her old husband's grandchildren. And so family relationships grow, sometimes inextricably inter-linked.

My grandmother had herself given one of her daughters (by a third husband, it is true) in marriage to the youngest grandson of her first husband: so that this young man had married his aunt (his father's step-sister) and this near incest had provoked many jokes. Similarly, my uncle's wife had been chosen from among these same offspring, always because of the old lady's obsessive insistence on strengthening the links with her first marriage. So, the new bride – this daughter-in-law who was brought into our family and who would one day assume all the domestic powers – was the great-granddaughter of my grandmother's first husband; she had always addressed the old lady by the respectful title of 'Lalla' ever since she was a child. Now, at the age of twenty, she became her great-grandmother's daughter-in-law!

These complicated alliances were the subject of the afternoon conversations. Other paradoxical aspects of blood relationship were explained by the women. As if they could not forget the fact that their daily existence was so impoverished of interest. As if the house became the whole city; I lingered there well past twilight; a scolding awaited me when I arrived home, escorted through narrow, dark alley-ways by a male cousin.

The women would take up the theme the next day or two days later. So-and-so, one of them would affirm, turned out to be both the half-brother and uncle on his mother's side of a certain lady, who just arrived on the scene with her hands full; and she would go off into a peal of laughter. When first cousins married, their children, another woman would explain, were both the nephews and brothers-in-law of their aunt; the game of incongruous family relationships inspired fits of uncontrollable giggles, sudden silences, attacks of nostalgia.

Men were thus brought into the picture by the ties of blood. Except for these discussions, they were identified solely by their daily occupations: some were artisans, others shop-keepers; while some were celebrated for their piety, others were common or garden sinners – drunkards – for whom the whispering women conjured up nights spent in dissolute debauchery in a red-light district of the city.

I pressed my face against the balustrade, absorbed by the old house which was gradually falling into decay. Twenty years on, I can feel the stillness of this tea hour yet; old ladies and young wives would emerge from their siesta, in ancient outfits, displaying all their jewellery; the adolescents would sit in a circle, models of decorum; the younger children would rush in, abandoning the games they had been playing in the corridors. Each guest brings her copper tray, glasses for tea, the coffee-pot and the dish of honey cakes.

Every day, at the same time, the idle gossip would be resumed, interspersed with stifled laughter, with tittle-tattle about the neighbours. Chatter punctuated only by the tireless hum of the seamstress's Singer . . . Suspense reflected in the mosaics, under the drooping jasmin. The fountain is dried up, the goldfish have disappeared. The interval draws to its inevitable close, in the shadow of the ancestor whom we imagine buried beneath these many-storeyed arcades that have lost their former glory.

'Shall I go up on the terrace?' a young girl murmurs.

'Will there be dancing tomorrow at the neighbours' circumcision party?' a divorcee asks, anxious to exhibit her jewellery.

'The musicians are expected, but perhaps they'll have been instructed to play only religious songs, you know how pious Fattouma is!'

When I was a little girl, I used to sit around at the feet of the embroidery woman, I would pass the seamstress her thread and scissors. I half-listened to the conversations: the important thing was to let them re-echo in my mind for years to come, the years when these women would continue to be cloistered. I lived subsequently outside the harem: my widowed father sent me to boarding-school, but I felt myself permanently linked to these prisoners.

I scarcely understood it at the time, but shortly before these gatherings, bitter words spilled out in the inner chambers: a mother's admission of rebellion, an angry wife's monologue after her master has gone, another's sobs and wailing as she lies helpless on a bed of sorrows, the sighs of a sterile spouse, whose husband has taken a second wife.

That concert of docile women, so ready to revolt, those dithyrambs of harsh words hurled in the face of fate, that threnody of woe, all remained relegated to the interior of the house, as veiled as the bodies of each woman without. That is why, as each of them left her chamber for these meetings on the patio, she wished to take full advantage of the light of heaven, as if this were an ultimate reprieve.

Two decades later, those women's bitterness finally overtakes me. Are they desperately seeking solidarity with each other, in this open space, where the peace has not been disturbed for centuries and gestures are age-old? The patio is not completely enclosed and light streams in. I remember the chorus of protest when one of the nephew-uncles proposed to cover it in with a glass roof, in order to show off his newly-acquired wealth. As each of the women was heir to an infinitesimal share of the dwelling, they had voiced their opposition. The men-folk of the family, artisans, fishermen, erudite exponents of the faith, all stood their ground in the vestibule, 'No glass roof, no glass roof!' they confirmed. 'We must keep one patch of sky!'

'That patch of sky has haunted me all my life!' groaned a divorcee, who was known to be sickly and whose husband had taken custody of her son.

Were these women trying to sweeten their arid destiny by means of the honeyed semolina cakes, by the ritual distribution of hand-embroidered napkins and the aroma of coffee whose quality gave rise to endless discussions? They bent their painted faces towards each other to tell their tales, and wisps of hair escaped from their striped head-scarves . . .

Patios of oblivion! When I come to kiss Meriem good-night, as she tosses about in bed, I muse on that kingdom to which you, the concubine, belong, and I draw new strength from addressing you so intimately: are you not, in your own way, familiar with these periods of waiting? . . .


I shelter behind the silence of so many anonymous women who remain hidden from sight. Is it to mitigate the failure of my old defiance? A couple; the novelty of the illusion fascinated me . . . I was driven to seek so many new horizons! I grew to rely for support on the presence of the man I loved, I who had escaped from confinement by pure chance. He became my *alter ego* . . .

When I returned from abroad, I chose to take refuge with an aunt who used to occupy a place of honour in my native city. She lives in an old house in the capital.

'I need a place to sleep, so I've come to you!'

'Of course, my darling! It was I who washed your mother's divine body before her burial. Is it not written that you return to your own kith and kin? May the widows of the Prophet intercede for us both on the day of resurrection!'

I have not stirred from the room whose balcony overlooks the harbour and the terraced slopes of the historic city. A flowering jasmin shades the french window. I lie on the mattresses piled up on the red tiles and daydream.

At midnight, when sleep eludes me, the next day during the siesta, memory revives my former aspirations. And it was there that I eventually began to speak to you, Hajila, the stranger, whom others imagine to be my rival, but who is my intimate. I also decided to get my daughter back.


Far from the hum of this metropolis, you remain a guest in your new home. People think you are a governess to those two motherless children, or a companion to an impotent man – you really don't know yourself. In fact, you are continuing my path through life, which I had assigned to you.

That morning I embraced my aunt. She wept at the affection of my greeting. In my infancy she had acted as a mother to me, until the day when – I could not have been more than ten – my father (whom she accused of being 'jealous of my love') preferred to send me to boarding-school.

'Why didn't you come back home, that year?'

She did not want to refer to my divorce, but wept for it as if it had been a death: 'All alone, so far away, on foreign soil!' she cried.

'I needed to reflect, and for that I needed to be out of doors! To walk, to look strangers in the face. I needed to be out of doors, but to be forgotten! In a manner of speaking, to be annihilated!'

In the evening, I resumed, 'Here, in this country, they annihilate you by shutting you up behind walls and windows hidden from view. No sooner do you set foot outside than you feel exposed! Over there, no one looks at me, no one really has eyes!'

I explained that I needed to work, to teach, but especially to have time for myself! Yes, I had given up – but not 'abandoned' – my daughter; her father was returning home and wanted to remarry, he'd put forward his proposition: 'A woman who'll look after the house and the children – that's all I want!'

'But what went on between you?' the old lady mumbled. 'They said you'd run off and that was why he kept the child!'

'Yes, I did run away . . . I wrecked everything!'

'I thought you were so happy! Every time you visited us for the summer, I was so proud to see you. I told my neighbours, my nieces, "May my brother's daughter find protection! Marriage suits her, even in foreign parts!" Only a year before . . . It was tempting fate!'

'I did run away,' I repeated. 'Now I've returned and I'm taking Meriem back. I thought she'd be happy with her father and brother and her father's wife who remains at home!'

'A step-mother!'

'No aunt! The trouble is with her father, I think!'

She thought I was still concerned for the man I had rejected. No . . . If my daughter hears no laughter in her home, how can she grow up? I had imagined that her father would find a child-bride, who would bring with her a never-ending source of carefree gaiety!

I had tried to keep my distance in order to break with the past. I had lightened my burden during my wanderings through cities. Meriem had written to me. I had hurried back; I could not free myself on my own.

# 13

# THE DRAMA

Here am I speaking to you again, Hajila. As if, in truth, I were causing you to exist. A phantom whom my voice has brought to life. A phantom-sister? Do we find sisters only in prisons – the prisons that each woman erects around herself, the fortresses of ecstasy . . .

The more my words outstrip me, the more my present existence dissolves; and your figure intrudes. My freedom of movement is only apparent: butterflies flying free at dawn, whose wings will crumble. Infallibly, fingers will reach out, destroying as they touch.

The man. I see him that last evening, howling in distress. Impotent. You will say 'knotted'. On his hands the stain of death.

My concern now is with the imminent drama. Our two lives merge: the body of the man becomes the party wall separating our lairs, which house a common secret.


After my daughter left, you felt, if not relieved, at least delivered from her gaze. When, in fact, she was waiting. For what? For your strength, no doubt. You read irony in her leisurely stare. Naïveté lends this dullness to the eyes. Meriem followed all your movements, fell silent when you entered a room, appeared to be on the alert. She was waiting for you. You imagined she was spying on you . . . As if a woman, even a child-woman, could spy on another woman! Unless it be on herself . . . Turning pensive eyes on her own destiny.

So, when the child disappeared, you felt liberated. Nazim could become your fellow-conspirator, be your son . . . You began to come home later and later from your excursions. The lad was always waiting for you at the door, he stared at you: your crumpled veil was lying askew. You would remove it nervously in the vestibule. You felt no need to warn the child. He would say nothing to the master.

One day, the two of them were waiting on the landing: Nazim in tears, and the man tight-lipped. You half smiled. 'Well, well!' you said to yourself, 'The man hadn't got the key of the house today? So I left my lord and master waiting at the door of his own home! . . . He'll be taking me back to the shantytown this very evening!' You refrained from expressing these thoughts aloud.

Nazim went to his room without a word; he didn't even emerge for dinner.

'How long have you been escaping like this, every day?' the man began in the glaring light of the kitchen.


He sits drinking by himself for a long time. One hour or two; maybe three. You don't sit down; you walk to and fro; you avoid passing in front of him; you walk round behind him. You go out of the kitchen; you walk down the passage; you come back in; in fact you are waiting. You don't stand idle. You find things to tidy up, in spite of the late hour; in a confused way, it seems urgent to leave the place clean and tidy, no strands of wool lying around, no coffee-spoons that haven't been put away, not a single speck of dust. As if you were leaving. You will be leaving, but will it be soon, during the night, or early the next morning? Eventually, you turn to watch the images unfolding on the television; the sound is switched off. The boy is asleep; he must surely be asleep . . . The television set is a recent purchase: for the news that the man watches every day. He switches off afterwards; sometimes he leaves the set on, but without the sound, like today.

The picture disappears. The screen flickers then goes blank. You crouch down for a moment on the floor behind the man's broad back; you pick up some knitting that you had left there, in a work-basket. The husband can't see you; you hope that he'll finally say, 'Come to bed!' What are you afraid of? You didn't dare go to the bedroom and be the first to get into bed. Will you have to pack your case before or after? After what? It'll take no time at all to collect your things, your clothes. Since you were only in transit here! As always; here or elsewhere.

The master hasn't moved. You can't hear him drinking now.

Eventually you're convinced you'll be there till morning. You wait.

Suddenly he starts grumbling; you can't understand a word. You don't get up; your fingers cease their movement to and fro, still grasping the wool. The man opens a bottle; he begins drinking again. The sucking noise of his lips is magnified in the stillness. Then he deigns to explain why he buys only this particular brand of beer; an imported brand, bottled locally. At least three times dearer. It's worth it for the quality. He compares it to other brands: its alcohol content, its lightness, taste. His voice drifts again into an incomprehensible mumbling: the words of a person talking in his sleep; you feel you are part of a nightmare. Without the terror, but with that sense of weariness rather, and the hollowness of everything.

The smell of beer sickens you, Hajila, as it does me. You make an effort to tolerate it. Afterwards you have to wash your hands and face and rinse out your mouth, even if it's the other person who's drinking; open the window, put the lid on the dustbin overflowing with dirty bottles; remove the stained sponge used to mop up the spilled liquid. And still the smell clings to your hands that the man never holds, and your lips that he never touches. It seems to be there for ever.

It is past midnight, or one in the morning. All the radio programmes have finished: in Arabic, Berber, French. The man has opened the last bottle, emptied it and flung it with a grand gesture towards the dustbin, from where it rolls on to the floor bumping along, exaggerating its own echo. Then he calls out, he calls me – you get up, move over to him.

'Isma! . . . Isma!'

You flatten yourself against the window-frame, waiting, aghast. Who is this strange woman who reappears, conjured up by his voice? You recoil. The master's voice is low, toneless. You wonder what is happening, death in your heart. You look at him, scarcely listening to what he says. You don't even feel any pity. You'd slipped on a dark woollen dressing-gown again, over your nylon nightgown . . . Eventually he catches sight of you; there's a glint in his jaundiced eyes.

'So! You've been going out for quite a time, Hajila "the runaway"?'

His tone is not sarcastic. He gets up, takes one step forward, and for you this is the beginning!

Like you, I have lived through fifty beginnings, fifty interrogations, I have faced fifty charges! Like you, I thought I had been responsible. I had tried to provoke him by my words! The confusion of words, spinning their snares in space, in the face of the unvarying folly of the male! . . . From time immemorial, the matriarchs have tried to teach us to stifle our voices. 'Keep silent,' they used to recommend, 'and never admit to anything.'

Throughout this caricature of a trial, I watched the ghost of a great love being flaunted, the trophy that I had carried through the streets. In the sunlight!


The sun is watching you, O Hajila, as you stand in for me tonight. While you secretly observe this man in the half-darkness, trapped in the web of his impotence, you begin to realize that he can do nothing. Nothing! Whatever he may say, whatever blows he may strike (for he will strike you, reviving memories of the miseries of the shantytown: pictures from your past surge up before your eyes – women moaning in neighbouring courtyards, some half-resigned to the brutality, some defiant . . .), however agitated the man may become in this new kitchen that is like a tomb, he can do nothing, nothing! But, most important, he cannot rob you of the thrill of the outdoors – the harvest brought back from your wanderings.

'The only reason why I'm not out of doors now,' you would like to say softly, 'is because it's dark! Let us imagine days which have no nights, O my sisters! Dusk would merge with dawn! The man would remain in this kitchen, soaking himself in alcohol and potions, while I would never weary of the world! . . . And the sun watching me!'

When he struck you, it was at daybreak or in the pale pre-dawn light . . . You had not heard the faint distant hum that heralded the day's stealthy approach. The man had left the light on: the bright circle in the middle of the ceiling cast elongated shadows; trapped by these four walls, you took a step towards the man, who had sat down again. You remained standing. His bare chest seemed even broader, his biceps white in the white light, his reddened eyes looking almost black, as if foreshadowing some insidious fever.

He began his interrogation, this prosecutor for the night and all the other nights. He asked you to sit down, in an apparently calm voice; you did not move; you did not understand. He plied you with a sudden burst of questions, still not violent: 'Who did you go to meet, when you went out? Who did you talk to in the public gardens? What strange man, what old or new friend accompanied you on these walks? . . . What make-up did you choose? What skirt did you wear under your veil, and why? What loud-coloured dress?'

You snapped back at him in monosyllables, feeling gradually disappointed at your own inability to invent any possible adventures to match those he was suggesting. How could you tell him that it was even more serious, that you were deceiving him with the faces of strangers, old men huddled up on benches, children hurtling about in play, how could you confess to the unquenchable appetite for more and more of these delights that consumed you every time the park-keeper's whistle announced closing-time in the gardens?

'What I liked . . .' you ventured.

'Yes?' He caught his breath, and a gleam of hatred flickered across his eyes and creased his eyelids.

'I liked to take off my veil in a narrow alley-way, when no one was passing, and then walk about naked!'

He struck at the word 'naked'. He struck blow after blow accompanied by the repetition of this word as if he recognized it. As if someone else had hurled it at him; it was I who had hurled it at him.

O, my sister from the shantytown, who has followed my footsteps into this tangle of misfortune, I used to walk naked when, as an adolescent, I first met this man! I went to high school and to university, but how was I to walk like this beside the man I loved? There was no tradition to serve me as a beacon.

Much later I was to jeer at him, 'Are men ever really naked? You are never free of fetters, you are bound fast by fears of the tribe, swathed in all the anxieties handed down to you by frustrated mothers, shackled by all your obsessions with some ill-defined elsewhere! . . . Show me one really naked man on this earth, and I will leave you for that man!'

I did better still, I left him for myself.

I taunted him, 'You have had me naked.' And I said triumphantly, 'I always made love to you with my body and soul stripped naked!' And I added ironically, 'The more you men swaddle yourselves, the more you think we women will be stifled!' It was too late!

For you also, it was too late. He strikes you across the face. You make no move to avoid the blow. He takes an empty bottle, breaks it on the edge of the sink and mutters, listening to his own eloquence, 'I'll put out your eyes and then you'll never see again! And no one will ever see you either!'

When he raises the broken bottle, you protect your eyes while calling on the Prophet; the blow catches you on the arm and the man stands, his hand poised, staring at the blood that spurts from the gash . . .

It is your turn to gaze at him wide-eyed . . . You have fallen back on the floor between the open door and the refrigerator. You hear him muttering now, far above you, at an enormous altitude, like a storm breaking on distant mountain peaks.

'I'll break your legs and then you'll never go out again, you'll be nailed to a bed and . . .'

Your whole body trembles spasmodically, as if powered by some interior clockwork, over which you have no control; nevertheless, you manage to mumble, 'The Prophet, the merciful Prophet will protect me! . . .'

The memory of Touma's monotonous voice echoes in your ears from out of the past: 'Your father! . . . A gentle man! . . . He never raised his hand to me. Never!' The other women would be moaning in the doorways of the neighbouring houses, 'Touma, tell us what to do! How can we protect ourselves from "their" brutality?'

'The Prophet,' you repeat.

And from the depths of your childhood, you can hear your mother's advice to them: 'Call on the Prophet who said all men of violence would be damned and no mercy would be shown to them!'

Suddenly Nazim rushes out into the passage, flinging doors open, sobbing, 'Mma! . . . Mma! . . .'

The father yells at him, ashamed that the child should see the beer bottles heaped up in the sink. You are forgotten, you, the prostrate slave, shivering uncontrollably, with your bare arms and shoulders.

'Get out, you son of a dog!' the man screams.

Nazim has opened the front door: the child who has adopted you, the little prince, the orphan in the snow, has gone to call on the

87

neighbours for help. He knocks at the other doors on the landing; the din re-echoes as in a dream.

Muttering curses, the man pulls himself together; he orders you to clean up the blood and go and hide yourself. You remain motionless as a statue – an effigy whose hearing is nevertheless acute. He busies himself trying to conceal what he deems to be 'the evidence of the crime' – the bottles.

A man has a right to go off the rails when he is drunk, but what punishment will the Apostles of the Revealed Law – that unwritten law – mete out to a woman who goes about 'naked', without her master's knowledge?

# 14

# THE WOUND

You do not feel the blow strike you, no pain thrust into your flesh, when your muscles tauten in readiness for headlong flight and help hold back your screams, lest you wake some sleep-walker in the night. Action speeded up or in slow motion, muscles refusing to obey, in the grey haze of insomnia, in the immediate galvanic shock of the wound. First you must just sink back, dry-eyed, into the healing lassitude that overcomes you.

It is the moment after the pain that you have to face. The real wound that cannot be healed! Wide-eyed you look around for answers. By staring into the void you hope to find out why . . . why the exile? As if the exile were something visible! As if an infinite wilderness of desolation stretched out before you . . .

'Why?' The question deafens you. The harm has come from without; its smile that tempted you to strip has been the cause of your expulsion . . . Your powers of thought are atrophied and your mind works slowly. You formulate ideas of rebellion: why did you submit willingly to the blow, when all you had to do was step aside? . . . You were too hasty in your dash for freedom, no one had warned you against the sun. It would have been so easy to put up some show: a rapid retreat, a temporary return to the harem.

Outside the house, you find that you are scarred with an indelible tattoo. You cannot weep; you regret the sweet relief of tears. But spurred on suddenly by desire for the world, you rush out of the room and leave the house. As you walk at random, with faltering footsteps, your eyes are free at last to look around you.

Derra: *the word used in Arabic to denote the new bride of the same man, the first wife's rival; this word means 'wound' – the one who hurts, who cuts open the flesh, or the one who feels hurt, it's the same thing!*

*Is not the second wife, who appears on the other side of the bed, similar to the first one, almost a part of her, the very one who was frigid and against whom the husband raises avenging arms? At which the first wife smiles, an ambiguous smile.*

*The man stands naked. The first wife slips away when the second enters, or makes her exit, only to reappear the following night: small consolation, the Book imposes on the polygamist the duty to bestow on each and every co-wife a strictly equal share of the nights of conjugal love. Small consolation! . . .*

*And the man, with no fixed abode, conveys himself each night from bed to bed, this* chassé croisé *continuing throughout the life of a male, from the age of twenty to sixty or seventy. So, the second wife laughs in her sleeve on the appearance of a third, who in turn will beat an apparent retreat when the fourth arrives. For, in our land, the man has a right to four wives simultaneously, as much as to say, four . . . wounds.*

# PART II

## DESTRUCTION AT DAWN

*Scheherazade said to her:*
  *'My dear sister, I need your help in a matter of great importance; I beg you not to refuse me this. My father is about to take me to the sultan, to be his bride! Let not this news dismay you; listen to me patiently.*
  *As soon as I am in the sultan's presence, I shall beseech him to let you sleep in the bridal chamber, so that I may still enjoy your company tonight. If I obtain this favour, as I hope to do, remember to wake me tomorrow morning, one hour before daybreak!'*

A Thousand and One Nights
(*before the first night*)

*As night falls on her nuptials, the sultan's radiant bride is accompanied by an attendant, her own sister.*

*'My dear sister,' Scheherazade begins, 'I need your help in a matter of great importance . . . My father is about to take me to the sultan, to be his bride!'*

*And Dinarzade agrees, even before the request is formulated.*

*'As soon as I am in the sultan's presence,' Scheherazade continues, 'I shall beseech him to allow you to sleep in the bridal chamber . . . If I obtain this favour, as I hope to do, remember to wake me tomorrow morning, one hour before daybreak!'*

*For the polygamist, any female blood relation of his wife is taboo, at least in the wife's lifetime. Is that why a man, be he sultan or beggar, threatens with death the woman he has possessed? Or, on the other hand, would this polygamy that excludes the spouse's kin be the only conceivable way for a man to find peace with every woman he desires?*

*In any case, Dinarzade, the sister, will be keeping watch near at hand: she will be close by while they embrace; she will look on at their carnal feast, or at least give ear to it. And the sultan's bride will be reprieved for one day more, then for a second; to be sure, the tales she spins help save her, but first and foremost it is because her sister has kept watch and woken her in time.*

*Assured of the sister's collusion in keeping sleepless watch, Scheherazade has been able to indulge in erotic transports, then yield to sleep. Awakened one hour before dawn, as if she had not slept, as if she had never known a man, she will give free rein to her virgin imagination.*

*To throw light on the role of Dinarzade, as the night progresses! Her voice under the bed coaxes the story-teller up above, to find unfailing inspiration for her tales, and so keep at bay the nightmares that daybreak would bring.*

*And all the fears haunting women today are dispelled, because of the two faces of the sultan's bride.*

# 1

# THE CHILD

The child lies under the brass bedstead which glints in the dim light of the room, under the double or triple mattress with its many coverings, draped in so many heavy hangings or light curtains of silk and net, redolent of rose-water or orange-blossom, all hand-embroidered by the virgins of earlier days as they spent their lives in waiting – under the bed where the couple copulate, as every night falls, the child hears the voice. Lying in the hollow of the cradle, suspended under the high bed, the child hears her mother's song drawn out through the night.

As every night falls the voice arises: first a faint murmur, a whisper, then a hiss – it falters, then slowly launches into a rich swelling song. The song of love's fulfilment.

The child under the bed hears and gradually falls asleep, lulled by the waves that break around her.

Sometimes the woman hesitates, falls silent for a moment, pitches her voice one tone higher, chokes on her words, then enters into an obscure dialogue. Once again the wave rises, the lament hangs momentarily in the air, as if the voice were piercing black depths of despair; it is heard again, preparing a response, it curves around, unwinding, seems to seek a confrontation, as if forced to harp indefinitely on the one string.

The voice closes in on a scarcely perceptible presence; it weaves its weft into the other's stillness, his silent listening. The woman's song isolates the shapeless man, the faceless father, whose oppressive weight on the bed makes the night indecent ... The child, open-eyed amid all this delirium, keeps time with the voice as it dances in jubilation. And every night rejoices.

The child hears the voice; later, much, much later, she will become a woman. Not on the first night, nor any of the early nights, but after she has travelled through the desert of familiarity, protected by continually moving on, her burden eased by her enthusiasms. Suddenly, out of the blue, her voice rings out.

As soon as the body sings, memory that had been hibernating for many long years revives. She is transported back to that place beneath the parents' bed.

The child hears the voice, the first voice of the woman in love who sings endlessly in a long corridor, hemmed in by the wall of the night. Transparent night. The languid, proud voice of the mother who thinks herself a queen.

The child, for the first time, hears the voice beneath the bed. In the secret of the nest, in this hidden corner of the night, in the warmth of this ignorance, the harem closes in on all of us women.

# 2

# THE SISTER

The brass bedstead is eventually auctioned, its brass fittings crushed and put out for sale on the pavement by the junk dealer. The voice beneath the bed is once again that of the woman who lurks there through the night to waken the sleeper on the verge of the new day.

Every night a woman prepares to keep watch to prevent the executioner's bloody deed. The listener now is the sister. Her vigil ensures that she will render without fail the promised assistance; she brings the hope of salvation before the new day dawns.

The sister waits beneath the bed. The favourite's sister; and she is there just because she is the sister, so taboo to the polygamist. The story-teller's sister, sister to the woman who has dreams and anticipates her fate, who is hailed as the sultan's bride for a day, and who knows that at sunrise she will be sacrificed and who, with every word she utters, hovers between extinction and the throne.

The master lies in the centre of the bed, with fixed eyes, the man interposed between woman listening to woman. A current flows from the story-teller above to the woman keeping watch below this stage – the setting for love.

The man who has the power of life and death listens. He listens as he carries the weight of the fatal verdict, which he suspends for twelve hours at the most, until the following dusk.

A woman keeps secret watch beneath the bed: a woman prompts the other with a word at the first sign of weakening. Her voice is ready to fly to the rescue, picking up every dropped stitch in the tale, and this woman is the sister.

But first of all she had had to let the sounds and ferment of amorous play flow over her head. The confused murmurs: a *wadi* in spate, even in the heart of the desert. Menacing, roaring, deadly flood waters.

But why does the sister take up her place beneath the bed? . . .
The law allows the polygamist to take any concubine, any female
slave of whom he is the master, except the sister of the woman
whom he tumbles in his bed. Thus, the sister beneath the bed can
lie in wait, hearing everything, and for that very reason, shield from
death.

She can take up her lodging in the morass of the others' sexual
pleasure and keep guard at the same time. Alone, under the
draperies of the divan, on which they sport, she lets their silken
sensuality slip past, and at the same time forestalls death's advance.
Alone, since she is the favourite's sister, her double and the one
who can never be her rival. Her duty is to waken; she is also the one
who snares the birds.

Up above, the sultan's bride spins her tales; she is fighting for her
life. Her sister, beneath the couch, rallies the past victims.

# 3

# THE COMPLAINT

The corner of the red-paved terrace is overhung with jasmin. Just opposite, the doors of the modernized kitchen and the huge, old laundry are always open. The water runs ceaselessly.

Every morning, the women wash down this spacious, light upper storey: the many long, narrow, shady rooms open out on to a covered, L-shaped vestibule. The terrace, which is wider, stretches as far as the neighbouring houses. A low wall marks its boundary; the children climb over it all the time to try to catch a glimpse of the sea and guess at the port in the distance, with its surging activity. Sometimes, a trawler appears on the horizon at first light, and its silhouette can be seen all through the long summer's day.

Girls under ten never venture into the new city. So they spend their time on the lookout up on the flat roof, daydreaming and keeping an eye on the comings and goings of the women of the house. They are haunted by the possibility of escape. 'My little quails, O my little brood, my future brides!' one of the ladies croons, in a wave of nostalgia, as she passes close to the children, before returning to her saucepans or her washing.

Before this, first thing in the morning, the girls had been out and about in the *medina*, running all the errands, calling at the nearest communal bakery or the local grocer's, going to the most humble *hammam* or visiting the countless members of the extended family.

Wedding days, when every alley and passage is inundated with throngs of veiled matrons, swarms of brightly-clad children, donkeys laden with baskets and victuals, groups of two or three itinerant musicians. On more ordinary mornings, the town crier, an old, corpulent Turk, follows his time-honoured route; with a ratatatat on his drum by way of prologue, he announces important events: a death, a circumcision, a forthcoming religious feast or

100

simply a meal that some charitable person is serving to the poor. He is the only man to raise his voice, whereas the muezzins, at the fixed intervals from dawn to dusk, bleat out their almost inaudible, whining calls to prayer, which the children promptly ignore.

Perched on the low wall of the terrace, the little girls peer out towards the sea: there, in the distance, boys can forgather with fathers and uncles, there, yonder, lies a forbidden theatre. Are the beer-drinkers dozing in the sun near the Roman statues? Dusty squares resound to yelling football fans, processions of singing boy-scouts stir up the provincial torpor. Oh! just to imagine bathing in the sea! Boy cousins return tired, glossy-haired, bright-eyed from their bathe, and hang their costumes to dry all day on the clothes lines on the terrace. Indications of a paradise so near and yet so far! Who can open its gates for us? The boys bring home sea-urchins' empty shells to tease us, as these are a delicacy decreed to be taboo for the female race! One boy describes the taste: long afterwards, the child that I was dreamed of the spicy words that lad used, as if it was not just one forbidden fruit, not just the sea and all its produce from which I was shut off. As if that boy were beginning to dream of his mother's sex and, out of bravado, revealing for me, and for himself, his own incestuous longings.

Other laments which lay hidden in these interludes of childhood, behind the screens through which the light of vanished summers filters, now erupt out of the past. Laments of unknown women, companions of my mother who died prematurely, uttered on one occasion only.

I must have overheard them by mistake. Carelessness on the part of the speakers. Every day's tally of misery, or its surfeit. Anger mounts, helplessness too much to be borne. Disjointed words of complaint are flaunted. Vain voice of discontent. I must have overheard by accident, or was it what I had to hear?

In the corner of the terrace overhung with jasmin, rows of huge braziers were lit just before dusk, on which saucepans brimful of different ragouts were soon steaming . . . Women stoop busily over them. Their long, jet-black plaits hang down below their waists;

their arms are bare, their faces flushed. They bustle around, urging each other on, uniting their efforts unhurriedly, they are worn out with so many guests to feed.

Down below, men draped in woollen or silken robes crowd into the ground-floor rooms, which open out on to the patio, with its black-and-white checkerboard paving; some prosperous and obese, others ramrod-stiff, encased in their ascetic scruples. They file in endlessly, each in turn leaving his slippers on the threshold. The hum of greetings, the murmur of interminable formulae of welcome or blessing. Dishes of semolina and spicy meats circulate, pitchers of cold milk, scalding-hot teapots change hands.

In the background, the lutes strike up their first chords. Is it a cousin's circumcision, the youngest uncle's engagement, my father's remarriage after being so long a widower?

Up above, the women-folk bustle to and fro, between terrace and laundry or kitchen, dovetailing their movements in a flurry of orders . . . The din of the crowd rises up in waves; a little girl, prowling around, peeps over the balustrade. This horde of worthies on the patio, who wipe their lips before embracing each other on the shoulder . . . Fascinated by so much ceremony, hidden among the skirts and *sarouals* of the women of the family, the child accidentally overhears an incongruous lament. She cannot see the face of the one responsible for the imprecations, there are so many busy hands and arms mixed up in the steam; one, two neighbours stand in front of the speaker, but the anonymous voice continues the lament:

'How long must I endure this life of drudgery, cursed that I am? Every morning, every day at noon, every evening, my arms are worn out rolling out the couscous! At night, no respite for us wretched women! We still have to suffer them, our masters, and in what an attitude!' – the voice quivers, interrupted by a bitter laugh – 'with our bare legs stuck up in the air!'

The complaint, in Arabic, spilled out in two improvised passages of rhymed prose. Striated words, that her shocked companions try in vain to hush. The prudes who fear this outburst of verbal fury. Which young aunt, which neighbour, with damaged soul, was expressing her revolt in these terms?

I never knew which one it was. Her shrill voice still echoes in my ears. The lament, with its echoing rhymes, is rooted in my memory: rhythms, sound and words. The movements of bare arms above the steaming victuals, choreograph some half-glimpsed drama.

Down below, the lutes and rebecks drone. The first lamps are lit, someone brings out a candle which sheds a red pool of light on the carpets. That lament dumbfounded me, suddenly robbing me of any future. As I withdrew to the wall of the terrace, I probably repeated those last words: 'And we still have to suffer them, our masters, and in what an attitude, with our bare legs stuck up in the air!'

The voice choked with anger, or in a final burst of derision. The prudish 'Sh! . . . Sh!' resumed. Was it a relative's hand that drew me away from the group? . . . Another, realizing I was eavesdropping – jolted out of her naïveté by the vehemence or stirred by the obscenity of the image – another voiced a reproach; I remember all the women then turning towards me in a chorus of surprise: 'Get the motherless child away from here! God will thank you! . . .'

I had understood nothing, as the image had unfurled in a black void, but this unanimous fear filled me with alarm.

Down below, the men's feasting continued. Perched on the low wall, I no longer had any desire to gaze at the skyline of the distant, unknown city; I could no longer envy the boy cousin who was showing off his sequined waistcoat – this detail confirms that it must have been a circumcision party: all this fuss and this crowd for a lad of seven or eight to have his foreskin snipped off! . . .

Long afterwards, one or two decades at least, I forgot the bitterness of the lament, the despair in the unknown voice in the midst of the long-past feast. I tried to suppress in myself the tenacious curse. The vanity of the protest must have made me abstain from fruitless indignation . . . Yet the jasmin continues to bring forth its fragile flowers, the bevy of stooping young women is still interwoven into the tapestry of my memory.

Today, to come to the rescue of a concubine, I imagine myself beneath the bed; alone, with the task of waking her, I revive the image offered long ago. That of the women – 'with bare legs' – the women who are expected to be lovers at night and who become slaves as soon as the sun rises . . . Will the tale of the sultan's bride save one of these oppressed women? The words of a faceless woman, bent over the fire on the terrace in my childhood, these words spilled out in an inexorable lament, in a twilight tarantella. And the motherless child preserves them, the scars of the wound, to intone them on the pillow of an impossible love . . .

# 4

# THE KISS

A proud family that has seen better days and is now reduced to austere economy, has its home in the mountains amid scorched olive groves, lentisks and agave flowers, where the hillsides are blackened in summer from forest fires; there, far from the sleeping city, the flute never ceases its lament, the shepherd whines his plaintive dirge, the rhythm of a stray tambourine haunts the forest. Then the child remembers and the vagabond dancing-women make their appearance.

No matron will tell her whence they come; they settle near this *douar*, for one day or one week, no male keeps the tally; they appear in groups of three or four, just enough to put on their nightly hypnotic show, beyond the meagre trickle of the *wadi*, behind the reeds and oleander bushes, while those whose pious principles bid them stay behind in the farmyards, together with the keepers of the *zaouïa*, lower lustful eyes.

No one even knows where these women stay, as they never sleep. The whole night through, they dance and prance, wriggling their plump hips from time to time, never moving their shoulders and keeping their necks quite stiff, like nautch-girls from some former festivity. The peasants crowd around, their gleaming pupils glued to the dancers' bellies and tossing hair. They do not even sleep in the daytime; they vanish at sunrise, gypsies wandering whither?

The child remembers the mountains where these goddesses appeared.

Later, much later, I encountered them again at the *hammam*, encased in silence, and I realized they were the inmates of a neighbouring brothel, close to a military camp. The same or their sisters, finishing their personal adventure in these narrow cities on the seashore. Their eyes were extended with kohl, their features dulled 'by debauchery and alcohol' (according to the honest citizens who pulled their brood of children away); their tunics were faded, but their naked, perspiring bodies were adorned with a mass of flashy gold jewellery, which they wore from steam-room to tepid chamber.

As soon as they entered the vestibule of the Turkish baths, I recognized them for the disfigured victims that they were. In the wake of these outcasts, who were a mixture of vulgarity and hauteur, I could hear once more the rhythms of Bedouin songs: I could hear the *nay* sound again behind the hills, even through the din of the crowded baths. For me, they were straight away metamorphosed into pagan princesses.

As a little girl, during one of the summers when the whole family left their home in the city to visit the rural sanctuaries of the ancestors, I had caught my first glimpse of the dancing-women. I recognized them. A lost dream, a star reborn that resumes its course across an ink-black sky.


I couldn't say whether my mother was still alive or not. We used to go back every summer to her family's mountain retreat. As my grandfather had had two co-wives (he had been killed just before his eldest daughter's death), my mother's step-mother, whom I now discovered, as well as numerous aunts barely older than myself, was still a young woman, with a gentle, open face. These childhood outings brought a taste of freedom.

My mother succumbed to tuberculosis. After her death, our trips to the *zaouïa* took on the nature of a pilgrimage. My father, grave-faced, accompanied our band of city-women: we travelled in two barouches which we hired in the town, and when we reached the end of the 'Roman road', we proceeded on foot, with the exception of my grandmother – she was visiting her rival, with whom she was reconciled when their husband died – who arranged for a horse to meet her. She rode in front of us, bolt upright, prouder than ever when one of the tenant-farmers turned up to walk beside her, holding the leading-rein. And so we all climbed up to the *zaouïa* which we reached before the extreme heat of midday.

I can remember those annual caravans which continued every year until I was about ten. It is as if the same procession were filing interminably past in my memory. I can see my father's tall fez in front of me, standing out strangely among the head-scarves of the mountain-folk and villagers. The last year, he had decided to buy a Citroën, to make our journey easier, but my memory has obliterated any further visits; the flute had ceased to rally the Bedouin dancing-women.

We arrived at the home of our peasant relatives. Whitewashed rooms opening on to orchards, where large stables became my kingdom. The women here seemed more given to laughter, as if they never left childhood behind, but suddenly, without transition, became immeasurably old and authoritarian. I was moved by their simple gaiety, as I was by the smells of the place; in the unpaved courtyard, overhung by vines, I let the solitary night envelop me.

I must have crept out one evening, when the reed-pipe called. Somehow, I found myself outside the hedge of fruit-laden pomegranates and mandarins. I wormed my way among groups of strange men, mostly crouching in the half-light. Suddenly, I could see the glittering, moving bodies, and multi-coloured scarves of three dancing-women. Someone pulled me violently away and took me to my father. He was sitting in a more respectable circle, not far away, talking to some elders. He beckoned to me quietly to sit and wait beside him, when suddenly . . .

An old man, with an unkempt beard and glittering eyes, with the eccentric look of an itinerant beggar, broke through the circle and stood facing me. He whispered a few words to my father who smiled faintly. As if giving tacit permission. The stranger immediately bent down in front of me and seized my hands, almost violently.

'Allow me to kiss your hands,' he said aloud, as the circle of men went silent. 'O, little one! You are the bearer of your ancestor's *baraka*!'

He studied my face for a long time, as if aware of my confusion, then, still tightly grasping my hands, he brushed his lips over them. Then he let go, jumped up, turned on his heels with youthful energy, and disappeared with a flourish into the night.

My father drew me gently against his knee, to reassure me. He resumed his conversation, as if nothing had occurred. Soon after this, the astonished women told all around about this incident; one of them reproached me vehemently for having wandered into the company of men 'at my age'. I was only six – or possibly seven.

I discovered that in this rural society, at least among those who think themselves the elite, the taboo falls on every female child of this age. It is true that in our city, whose population had been increased in the sixteenth century by Andalusian refugees, girls were confined to the harem when they reached puberty, but that was not till they were eleven, twelve, or sometimes thirteen. Immeasurable progress! . . .

For this strange man, who greeted me as the bearer of blessings, I was first and foremost the heir to the maternal line. By virtue of this, I was the descendant of the saint in the hills, a *sufi* who had come from the eastern frontier of the country to these mountains that had once been green. This traveller had left the confines of the desert and the ocean, to settle in these valleys, taking numerous wives and receiving homage and many offerings before dying, full of honour. He bequeathed his powers to a new saint, his grandson probably, though some said his nephew: just as in the case of the Prophet, God seemed deliberately not to have given him a male heir.

The two sanctuaries, of the Old Saint and the Young, stood side by side in an olive grove. For four or five centuries, their heirs – at that time without exception from father to son – traded in this *baraka*. It was their livelihood. They considered themselves more and more as mediators. Down to my mother.

Then the break suddenly occurred, at least in the eyes of the old man I had glimpsed. Whence the magic of that kiss. As if he was the first to state, in the presence of witnesses and near to those lascivious hypnotic sessions, that I could become a priestess. For the first time, it was up to women to uphold the tradition of the Word and prophesy . . . The bearer of this annunciation vanished as quickly as he had appeared. For that very reason, no one disputed the legitimacy of the homage he paid me; but inside the overcrowded house the women affected to be shocked by the fact that I, with the obliviousness of a town-dweller, had been in a masculine gathering on a night when the hetæræ were in action!

I made much of this kiss, this oath of allegiance. Not forgetting my father's faint smile which had authorized it.

Later, as an adolescent, in the absurd haste of the times to 'modernize' Islam, I came to disparage peasant superstition. Because it claimed to make me assume the problematical blessing of mummified ancestors, while my exposed body could only denounce, by its freedom of movement, the curse which weighed on every woman around me . . .

I tell myself today, now that I have passed through the tunnel of enforced silence, that my hands alone were protected; because an unknown beggar had brushed them with his lips, they were attached, by some obscure link, to the spiral of the past.

# 5

# THE OUTCAST

My childhood home was in a narrow alley where houses huddled close together allowed everyone to spy on everyone else. Especially since some families had had windows put into the ground floor, as a concession to the French custom. One woman in particular, a childless widow named Lla Hadja, was reputed to be a terror for tittle-tattle.

The lady was rich. She was said to have been able to afford the pilgrimage to Mecca, at least twice or three times. She had returned loaded with gold, head-bands, shoulder-sashes, sequined belts that she wore in the morning, while she sat enthroned at her half-open shutters. Behind this screen she kept watch every minute of every day: pedestrians, visitors, every passer-by knew she was there; they could hear her cough during the siesta as well as in the cool of the evening.

As the mornings stretched out endlessly – men hurrying from the house, children standing around playing or daydreaming, veiled servants leaving on furtive errands – Lla Hadja not only kept guard, she presided over this street spectacle.

Calling to a lost child, crying forlornly on the pavement, summoning a little girl carrying home trays of galettes, brown bread, cinnamon buns on her head, the lady's voice rang out close at hand . . . As if the wall did not exist, as if the window, although closed, projected into the street or was a royal balcony. The lady would expostulate vigorously; the lady would chide good-naturedly; everyone knew she was sitting there, an upright, scented, imposing idol whose every word and every call reverberated through the air.

Some people went so far as to bruit it around that she had participated in her youth in God knows what drinking sessions with certain long-dead notables. So much so that her supercilious severity towards others, the untiring zealous watch she kept, was simply her repentance, secret anxiety for her own salvation, that three or four decades had not allayed! Certain people went so far as to suggest, but only in hushed whispers . . .

From dawn to dusk, she kept her eye on this street which I knew so well: no woman escaped her vigilance – none of those who briefly, illicitly, furtively slipped their shackles for an hour or for a day.

The only women who were preserved from this supervision were those who, by virtue of a high-ranking father, brother or husband, never left the house – where the master, on installing a private harem in his domicile, took pride in the total invisibility of his women-folk. Not to be seen by Lla Hadja seemed to be the most exclusive form of 'chic'! Her insinuations, her punning allusions, her proverbs, her rhymed comparisons on so-and-so, in brief, her every dictum was collected like an oracle and peddled in the public baths, in the cemeteries, in the markets where the country-women, come to sell their eggs and poultry, asked the servants for her latest pronouncements.

I must tell you that this one woman – Lla Hadja, whom some called 'the barren' – concentrated all her venom on one special victim, who was linked inseparably by rumour to the gossipmonger – a young woman whom I did not meet till much later, but who, for some mysterious reason, was nicknamed 'the outcast'. A name which seemed to veil the veil itself of the unknown woman.

I came across this woman in the capital. I was twenty, she seemed to be fifty; her face was buried in white organzine veils, which emphasized her reddish Berber complexion and made her narrow green eyes, with only the faintest outline of the habitual kohl, seem even deeper. She carried herself somewhat stiffly; a deliberate severity shut in her gaze. A slight flutter of the eyelids; long, delicate, pinched nostrils – I hurriedly noted these details, perceiving the genuine goodness, the hidden nobility of the person in her modest reticence, which her conspicuous skin colouring belied. Yes, that day I was seeing 'the outcast' from my street, at least fifteen years after I had left it.

In that same street, no matter how hot the day, Lla Hadja's vigilant

111

eye continued to follow the comings and goings of every passer-by: the trader, making his punctual way towards his stall, the lad returning from the *medersa*, and most of all, yes, most of all, those lingering veiled ghostly figures. There were girls approaching puberty who began by muffling head and shoulders in a short folded cloth, then those who, once they turned twelve, disappeared for good into the darkness, from which they emerged only to go for the weekly bath – when they clumsily experimented with the art of the veil and its subterfuges – all these victims of the first stage of close confinement excited the matron's attention as she sat enthroned, impassive behind her shuttered windows.

Lla Hadja inspected out of habit the other daily apparitions: a Berber tunic that seemed so out of keeping on these white silhouettes, or the coarse veil worn by would-be towns-women. She noted the casual skill with which a passer-by lifted the cloth up to her thigh, she observed fingers folded on the chest or under the chin, glimpsed the eyes with lowered lids, the perfect arch of eyebrows, and half of a brow emerging from under a satin head-dress which covered the roots of the hair.

She left nothing to chance: she could identify any woman passing by, whether her drapery be of silk or wool. She would recognize the mature woman by her *babouche*; the refined bourgeoise by her rather delicate mule; the pious woman by her slipper and, on rare occasions, she would spot a westernized coquette by her court-shoe . . . Lla Hadja could immediately put a name to the silhouette – the surname, sometimes also a forename (so-and-so's second, or fourth daughter-in-law or aunt and her place in a certain domestic hierarchy) until the silhouette, shrouded in its veil which was supposed to rob it of its identity, disappeared out of the street and into the darkness, as night fell.


'The outcast': I ran across her again in the capital, in the visitors' waiting-room at the Barberousse prison. Even in this new setting, under these ignominious circumstances, this crowd of women – cousins, distant kin, visitors laden with food and entrusted with messages – congregated in separate groups according to the town they came from. While I waited my turn, among all the different families coming and going, someone pointed her out to me; it was the same woman, crouching down now on a doorstep, her face partially hidden by her little veil, bowed down by the weight of infinite patience, beyond that of resignation or hope. She resembled a saint in a Persian miniature, this prison visitor who might have remained anonymous, and who, I was told, was that same woman who had been driven out of the street I had lived in as a child. An apparition strangely neutral, both mystic and transgressor.

I had pieced her story together from stray allusions, odd words dropped with a wink and a nudge, whispered fragments of confession, never from any first-hand accounts, and even less from those who had played an active part in the drama, which had lain so long concealed: fifteen years before, she had been forced to leave her home, virtually driven out by a younger brother.

It was as if this woman, whom I came across again in that prison entrance, and on whose features, lit by an aura of meekness, life's wear and tear had left scarcely a mark, so that in age she still retained a childlike look, it was as if this stranger who was yet so familiar, when I eventually came face to face with her, brought to life the only love story that had beguiled my childhood! 'Here at last is the heroine,' a melancholy inner voice began. A heroine who preceded any plot, the denouement having occurred before the conception of the story, of any story! So here was the woman who had been exiled for the crime of having wished to love!

A brief affair. Not even a ripple on the surface. An incipient flutter of emotion which caught the eye of the busybody behind her shutters, who amplified and multiplied it and the rumour was let loose, spreading fast, far too fast . . .

A young man of about twenty-five turned up again in his home-town after ten years' absence, in the street he had left without a penny and where he had since been forgotten; he now returned with a little nest-egg. He bought over for his widowed mother the house which was in joint family ownership, to the mortification of paternal uncles and cousins who had hoped to evict her. The young man is on holiday and without a care in the world. As soon as it's light, he goes down to the harbour; he mixes with no one, the only familiar thing in this crumbling city is the sea. He bathes every day, and returns in the early afternoon, carrying his bathing costume, slowly dragging his sandalled feet while the water runs down from his black, curly hair, over his youthful brow and his sunburnt face.

113

He passes Lla Hadja's window. Although he is a neighbour, he does not greet her; he does not formulate the slightest stereotyped expression of respect. He walks past stiffly, his thoughts elsewhere, healthily exhausted after his swim; the aura of his beauty leaves a silent, velvet wake. The lady says nothing; she continues to watch.

That went on for a month, or perhaps more. On the opposite pavement is a house that also has a window on the ground floor. A young woman lives there, married at sixteen to a man now old and ailing. Her brother occupies the first floor, where parties are always being held and the evenings are frequently enlivened by gatherings of women-folk with women musicians playing. The brother has made a rich marriage; the new bride, used to having her own way, creates a scene if she doesn't have all her clan around her. The husband is in love; his part of the house sometimes seems a trifle small; his sister, living downstairs, married to this invalid who has lost his job, is satisfied with her share of the inheritance.

She lives there with no children, with no future. She is twenty-one or twenty-two; six years after her marriage she returned like a bird of passage to this place with its seeping shadows. She is said to be scrupulously attentive to her sick husband. The newsmongers, who know that the brother had originally forced her to marry this man, praise her acceptance of her lot.

'What else could she do?' they conclude. Who, beside the brother, is master of a woman's fate when her marriage turns out to be childless?

And they bless her, after a pause.

Then the unexpected happens, or nearly happens. When exactly does the sacrificed sister, the disparaged wife, begin to peer through the slats of the closed shutters? Notice the young neighbour, whom she must have recognized, returning from the beach? Are they not almost the same age? Their families were so close! When did she suddenly recall, relive those childhood games, in which they both had shared? . . .

She was twelve or thirteen: she no longer crossed the threshold of her home, the only outlet for her carefree youth was sudden fits of laughter or incipient tears . . . She remembers now that the young man used to venture as far as the patio for a discussion with her brother, on some errand, or to bring a message. As children they had played on the same terraces and explored during the quiet siestas the dark nooks and corners at the end of the long street. Some people remember, will remember, the day when they were caught in the little garden of the church – that is of the mosque disguised as a church.

The warden, a vigilant Maltese, had seized the children by the ears and dragged them off to the school principal: pupils' truancies, especially those of Arab pupils, cannot end up in a churchyard! Someone today recalls the scene.

Was that the reason why the little girl was taken away from the French school? Suddenly house-bound, she helped her tuberculous mother who was wasting away; soon afterwards her brother married her off to a middle-aged man. She went to live in a nearby hamlet, but when her husband became an invalid (as a result of an accident at work probably) she returned to her brother's home, to fade away on the ground floor, a destitute, childless wife.


The unexpected happens ... or is it not to be expected? The taciturn young neighbour, now grown to maturity, henceforward walks past on the opposite pavement. No one sees him stop, even less knock and enter the house which was previously open to him. The only detail that can be observed is that he has changed pavements when he returns from his bathe. Lla Hadja is on the look-out. She imagines the young bather slackens his pace. Lla Hadja remains on the alert, at the exact moment when the young man passes the other window. Nothing.

And yet 'it' happens: how many times, I have been unable to ascertain. Lla Hadja declares that it is the woman 'possessed by the devil', 'the temptress' who whispers the first word.

Imagine Satan. Eve. A wife wandering aimlessly around an invalid's darkened house. Observing every morning the return of the man whose moist body brings with it the smell, the warmth of freedom. His regular step, as he passes, brings surging back the days of yesteryear, the fits of laughter in a doorway, or on a bench in that little churchyard. Every day. One morning she forgets herself – is she asleep, is she dreaming? – she succumbs, she quietly calls.

His name. His forename. So plaintively, so sweetly. He hears. He does not stop. Tells himself that the old lady opposite can hear. The eye is watching.

115

The young woman repeats her call. More softly. More anxiously. More touching than a tear that wells up unbidden. The next day, or the day after, the shutters which till then had remained closed, opened to let in a thread of light and maybe of hope. The sunburnt young man, with the black curls falling over his damp forehead, returns from his swim, dragging his sandalled feet, carrying his dripping costume, and the young man pauses for a moment. As if he had stumbled on a stone. He bends down slightly to look at the ground, perhaps to see if his foot is hurt.

The eye misses nothing. Lla Hadja has understood. That same evening, the rumour begins to grow. It becomes a long story, the first act of an intrigue. Lla Hadja, they say, understood all along:

'As soon as she called to him, I was on the look-out, I knew what to expect! When you send these girls so young to the French school, you must be prepared for anything! The devil is on the rampage, evil strikes. I knew, I foresaw this, I expected it. I can tell you, she managed to slip a letter to her lover! The sorceress! The barren wife! Poor, poor bed-ridden husband, whose wife has no pity!'

The slander spreads: from servants to women selling poultry in the market, to fishwives in the courtyards, to would-be townswomen, to cloistered bourgeoises. The rumour flies from terrace to terrace. The dream of a woman in love seems a challenge to their confined existence.

A few days later, the brother is informed by one of his cousins, or one of his wife's female relatives. 'Your sister', that scheming creature downstairs, who keeps so many rooms out of use, and while seemingly so humble prevents the house being given over to festivities!

The brother, assuming the role of the husband, claims to be dishonoured. He presides over a family council: an uncle by marriage, who is an official out on the plains, is summoned hurriedly from his outlying post; a paternal aunt, impoverished and timid, is also invited.

The brother will be lenient. He won't make matters worse. He simply wants his sister out of the town. Her departure will put an end to the disturbance caused by 'the affair'. The unfortunate husband doesn't have to know about it. The brother, who sits in judgement, will buy over her half of the house; as her protector, he will see that she finds accommodation elsewhere, in the capital, if she wishes. An excuse will be found in her invalid husband's need for urgent medical care. She will be decently housed. She can find employment doing embroidery for Mozabite traders.

She vanishes one morning: the woman who had sinned, who must be banished. Soon afterwards the young neighbour also leaves, returning to foreign parts. He'll never come back, 'to make trouble', Lla Hadja predicts.

After the young woman left, accompanied by her sick husband, did she ever think she had only herself to blame? To give rise to rumours, is that not a fault? Who will ask why she called to her former friend? Throughout the long years of arid existence, of the misery endured under the tyranny of her brother, at the dawn of every new day, every time she prostrates herself in prayer (for she has now become pious), she will ask herself: why? . . .

To have waited at the window for the young man's approach, to have flattened herself against the wall, to have hoped for that hesitant footstep, that silhouette which would open the door and slip inside, to have dreamed in the night of an embrace in the doorway, in the dim vestibule, to have remained glued to the shutters, as midday approached, throughout that wasted summer, to have wanted . . .

Suddenly, the brother and his tribunal. Before two witnesses, unyielding, but unashamed, silent, for she is suddenly aware of the surging desire that overwhelms her . . . In the next room the husband coughs, repeatedly calling her to bring him the spittoon.

'You have given rise to malicious gossip,' the brother begins. 'Your place is no longer here in the same house as my wife and daughters who, as they grow up, must not be sullied. How fortunate the man in the next room is, who, because of his illness will know nothing of this! If he had repudiated you, where would you have gone? Your husband protects your honour. You must wait on him like a servant, wherever you choose to live!'

'I shall go to the capital. Embroiderers from our town can always find work there with people who sell bridal outfits!'

'Everything will be done fairly!' he decides, while the witnesses chorus their approval, acquiesce ceremoniously, assure the brother of their respect, their admiration for his equity, for . . .

Years later, the story is evoked in elegiac fragments: what the brother did, what Lla Hadja said. Nothing more was known of the

117

woman who, one summer morning, caught the bus travelling eastward.

And so it happened that I recognized her in that prison waiting-room. She had become a prison visitor, at a time when the prison cells were so overcrowded; she came there out of piety or repentance. When her husband died she worked to be able to buy food, delicacies, with which she filled her baskets. She passed herself off as the aunt of a neighbour's son or of an acquaintance, and the prison officials didn't ask awkward questions. She visited men who had been sentenced, and she did it, so she said, 'for the consolation and the welfare of the faithful'.

# 6

# NUPTIALS ON A STRAW MAT

We children could get into the next-door house by climbing on to the low wall and jumping down on to the adjacent terrace. The oldest girl in this family had had a 'French-style' wedding: arrayed in a white satin gown, with two little bridesmaids in white tulle, holding a bouquet of orange-blossom – so that white became, not the symbol of virginity, but of entry into the Western world – on the morrow of a union consummated by force, with the brutality of rape.

Then the bride, flanked by the little bridesmaids in their fancy get-up, had posed for the photographer – the only man admitted to mingle with the host of female guests who had left their silken veils folded at the door as they arrived. Attired in low-cut gowns, well-nigh Parisian in elegance, they saw themselves sharing in the new ceremonial. Their comments – including those on the 'camera man', for whom this had been quite exciting – had been kept up well into the next few weeks.

The bride had been 'given' to a first cousin; but, thanks to a progressive evolution in customs, the second daughter could hope, as she herself said, to be able to marry for love.

This second daughter was a romantic soul. From the age of twelve, when she was taken out of school, to remain a recluse till her marriage, she had read avidly all the love-stories serialized in the fashion magazines to which she subscribed. She had even managed to get hold of several novels by Colette – the *Claudine* series as well as *Chéri*. She spoke in a hushed voice, she did not so much daydream as withdraw completely from the real world . . .

In any case, the local matrons lauded to the skies her skill in embroidery, dressmaking and lacemaking. They spoke with equal admiration of her beauty, her modesty (she blushed at the slightest word and never managed to make her tiny voice heard in the many social gatherings), as of her trousseau. Especially of her trousseau!

It combined the local Andalusian tradition and that of the European dream described by the French magazines. According to the former, the bride must arrive in her new home with a score of tunic-dresses in diverse colours, all embroidered with gold thread, and, in addition, everything for the conjugal bed-chamber: a number of mattresses of blond wool, which had been washed in surrounding streams, sterilized and compressed by indefatigable servants; counterpanes, drawn-thread-worked sheets, sequined cushions, hangings for the bed and curtains for the windows; and, lastly, the hand-embroidered toilet-bag for the weekly bath. But, like any European girl, she prepared an abundant wardrobe for herself: silk blouses, embroidered with drawn-thread-work (in Tunisian, Algerian or Moroccan style), short skirts and knitted pullovers. What is more, the second daughter, like her elder sister, had a right to the white gown for the great day – which however she would don only after she had appeared in the outfit consisting of garnet-red tunic, *saroual* with matching waistcoat, sequined sashes and flower-patterned mules. But she was not satisfied to order this immaculate gown by post and then make a few alterations. No, she cut it out herself, she embroidered it herself: last year she had regularly sat up half the night making this 'trousseau fit for a princess' with her own fair hands.

And every matron mused: how would she dare ask for the hand of this most beautiful, most sweet-natured, most gifted of virgins, for any of her sons? In fact, every one of these ladies feared the mother's uncompromising pride. It was well known that, in this family where sons had been born only after a brood of girls, the arrogant, strong-willed mother had eventually overshadowed the meek and reticent father.

So, nothing was lacking in preparation for the new nuptials, except the suitor. After the mother had rejected the seventh, the eighth request for her daughter, suddenly the news spread that the affair had been concluded. The second daughter had been 'given'. To whom? There were already equivocal smiles – not even to any son of theirs or anyone from the capital! Yes, a 'foreigner' had been accepted: to be sure, he was said to be a real scholar, a professor of something or other, some said of German, according to others it

120

was mathematics which he had studied in Germany up to a very high level!

That in no way diminished the stigma: the man was not a native of their town, nor even of any other town; he quite simply came from a nearby village. The two mothers had met at the Turkish baths, exchanged flatteries and become friendly. The gossips added that the two women had much in common, 'particularly their faults', shrilly asserted one neighbour. But in any case the match seemed to be serious with the suitor bearing the hallmark of a high official. The girl was lucky after all, that exceptional trousseau was in some way an omen: it augured a life of travel. And may Allah the All-Merciful protect her!

The first disappointment for the sisters – from the eldest who was already married, down to the fourth, a little girl who climbed over the wall to visit us – was the revelation of a custom thought to be obsolete: in the fiancé's native village, the marriage had to be performed according to the austere code of practice which the patron saint of the region had instituted some centuries before. It was known as marrying 'according to Sidi Maamar's Bough' . . .

This saintly personage had, in the days of old, preached against the ostentatious luxury of the inhabitants of the then prosperous cities. So he had set out the procedure for wedding ceremonies, down to the smallest detail. His disciples accepted the rule, not only obeying it themselves, but imposing it even more strictly on all their male offspring. If any of their descendants insisted on breaking the 'chain' it was noticed that children born of the union were without exception physically or mentally handicapped, unless they turned out to be ne'er-do-wells or jailbirds. This was proof that the saint's curse had remained alive over the centuries, and he was still vigilant down to the present day 'when aeroplanes fly and the radio speaks all by itself', as one of the pious ladies commented.

The fiancé's mother had explained. She could not go against the rule: the chain with them passed from father to son; she herself had suffered from such a ceremony 'almost funereal, as if she'd been an orphan, still in mourning', she had added . . . Thanks be to God, her daughters and her only son had turned out an honour and the joy of her heart, a light for her mature years, a beacon for old age!

So it would be for the new bride; she would suffer one night only – the first – of humility in obedience to the strict custom: in return would come the promise of blessing on her children who would be conceived 'beneath the bough of the saint'. A girl must be worthy of this opportunity for a husband like her son!

It seemed to us girls, as we listened to the youngest sister's story, that these people of peasant origin were quite amazing! Barbarians, disguised as city-dwellers, giving themselves over to magical practices, to primitive penances.

Certainly, we too acknowledged the saints' presence in our midst, with the matrons calling on them endlessly, at every turn in the conversation. Time and time again, they invoked their memory to heighten every discourse, on every possible subject, with the result that this familiarity seemed, by its very abuse, to be pure rhetoric, a mere stylistic device. As for controlling our day-to-day existence, our feminine love of ostentation, and dictating how our ceremonies should be conducted! No! Our men-folk were literate in Arabic as well as in French! Our sons might not go abroad in search of diplomas and degrees, but what was so grand about this if, meanwhile, the women trembled with fear like ignorant villagers? They might just as well live like the peasants they were and 'not mix with their betters', as one of our aunts had concluded peremptorily, with a gesture in the direction of the neighbours.

'Poor girl!' she added, 'I'm afraid that they are offering her as the sacrificial lamb to the herdsmen!'

'And what about Sidi Maamar's curse?' another asked.

'Islam is one, Islam is pure and unadorned! It allows you leisure for rejoicing! The law cannot change, it is the same, everywhere from our town to faraway Medina; I don't need any *fqih* or learned doctor from the *Zitouna* to explain it to me!'

But our neighbours had to comply. The girl prepared for her nuptials to take place beneath 'Sidi Maamar's bough'.


During the weeks before the set date, the women gossiping on the terraces every evening dwelt interminably on the details of the curious protocol.

No embroidered tunic, no jewels, not the slightest adornment for the bride on the wedding day, nor the preceding day nor even

122

during the ritual of the *hammam* two days before: at a pinch they might be permitted to wave candles and intone hymns during the evening ceremony, when the virgin's hands and feet were tinted with henna.

It was soon learned that only a token dowry had been given: one golden twenty-franc coin, which the bride was to save scrupulously and never spend. On the morning when the procession of barouches and cars arrived in our street, bringing the groom's female relatives from their hamlet, muffled up in their veils to escort the bride, there must be no clamour, no jubilant ululation, no music; at the most one old woman could hold a candle and recite some verses from the Quran at the exact moment when the match-makers stepped over the threshold.

These women would drink neither lemonade nor milk of welcome, they would not partake of a single date or the smallest almond cake. They would simply fetch away the virgin for whom they had come. She will have her face completely hidden and her body shrouded in a seamless cloth of wool or linen, so that she can neither see nor be seen by anyone, until her new master, alone with her at night, piously and solemnly removes the veil from her face: thus had the Saint Maamar decreed, four centuries ago.

And the gossipmongers mused at dusk: the bride would be conveyed like an object, gaze turned inwards, face bathed in tears, just fit to be buried! . . . What masochism, whereas fate, already so hard on women, did at least guarantee them the glamour of a wedding day!

This marriage promised to have nothing but misery in store. The gossipers were amazed, they protested that they'd never let a daughter of theirs make such a match, one might as well condemn the innocent maid to the grip of deliberate celibacy! It must be added that none of them was invited, only near relatives, as well as the female members of our family, as we were close neighbours.


I remember that wedding – or more exactly the morning after the wedding night.

The bride's mother had been in tears since the previous evening: no ululation, cakes not distributed (she hadn't been able to resist making them), the absence of professional female musicians from the town, the elegant, varied trousseau which no one had seen! She had decided to get her own back the next day, by displaying the luxury that had been forbidden the day before.

We set out before dawn to drive to that mysterious village: ten or so veiled women from the two adjacent houses piled into the van into which the mother had already loaded the trousseau, baskets filled with foodstuffs and the most delicate pastries. She would show those villagers, by preparing the wedding banquet herself, how refined her family was and what her daughter meant to her and all towns-women! The wedding celebrations would be up to the usual standards and the ascetic saint with his mortification of the flesh would have to take a back seat and let an older tradition be observed!

I can remember our excitement as we set out, still half-asleep, in the morning twilight, driving in the cold along the corniche, through the bluish mist. I remember our arrival at that house which was – well, what can I say? – just like any in the city – a building occupied by families of teachers from different regions. But, above all, I remember the bride, the moment we caught sight of her.

We entered the smallest room in the house, where mattresses were piled up on the bare tiles. There was total, tense silence, broken only by convulsive sobs coming from a white-shrouded heap huddled up against the wall, while a group of dumb-struck children clustered around, staring at the unidentifiable back. With an abrupt gesture, the mother chased the horde away. Only three women remained, I think, in addition to ourselves, the two little girls who were to be the bridesmaids – decked out in our white lace dresses and the shiny patent-leather shoes which seemed shockingly conspicuous in this setting!

The mother, with her woollen veil draped round her waist, stared for a moment at her daughter, huddled there, shaking with sobs. I have never forgotten the opacity of that silence. There was an enormous mirror facing the door, from which a large white sheet had just been removed and still hung down from one side. I could see the mother's reflection, seeming larger than life, as she stood with her face contorted.

'O my daughter! Grievous blow! Day of joy! day of woe!' she

declaimed, rhyming the Arabic words.

She gazed at her own image with a grimace of helpless despair and without even bending down to the bride, whose sobs suddenly ceased, she angrily, violently lacerated her own cheeks. Two female relatives rushed in and forced her outside (was it not a rule of the most basic modesty that mother and daughter should not be left alone the day after the wedding night, as if the intrusion of the man destroyed for ever the protection the mother could give to the virgin?).

'Shame on you!' one of the relatives chided.

'Have a care for your daughter's happiness!' murmured the other.

'Her destiny is only just beginning, do not be such an evil omen!'

The mother allowed herself to be dragged into the vestibule. We two little girls remained with one woman, probably the bride's older sister who had just slipped discreetly into the room, with modest bearing and anxious expression.

She sat down and put her arms round the bride who had resumed her convulsive sobbing after her mother's angry outburst. She crouched down beside her sister, whispering words of comfort, gradually encouraging her to give vent to her pent-up feelings, let her cup of bitterness spill over, say what hidden grievance sparked off this misery. Seated on a mattress, shocked by the mother's violence, I wondered what I should do. I felt ashamed of my incongruous white dress; should I listen, try to make out the cause of the bride's distress, see if it persisted, if? . . . The two sisters huddled together under the same veil, deep in whispered conference. At this precise moment, or perhaps later when the confession was resumed in snatches of conversation with other women in the town, I became aware of what heavy destructive footsteps had crushed the tender shoots in the dream garden.


The union had been consummated – for so the saint's code had decreed – on a simple sheepskin or a rush-mat: two bodies copulating under a blanket. Was it this uncouthness that caused the bride to sob so bitterly in the next day's first pale morning light?

She had to make her appearance in the afternoon, dressed in her finery, the tiara on her brow, but with swollen eyelids, and puffy-faced from the shock to her virginity.

'So,' commented her friends, who claimed to be in the secret, 'she wept because she didn't like the bridegroom!'

'Didn't like him?'

'He was too small, and probably an insensitive oaf!'

'Insensitive or unaffectionate?'

'What is affection in a man?' sniggered a malicious voice. 'Do our masters even know what affection is, since God has made all of us women, young or old, beautiful or ugly, to be like sheep, following at their heels!'

'Shame on you, with your bold, poisonous tongue!'

'What does it matter if the bridegroom is small and boorish?' retorted loudly another buxom woman. 'A man is a man! As long as he works to keep his wife and children and walks in the path of God, that alone is luck in marriage!'

'She didn't like him, she didn't like him!' the younger women repeated. They knew that this second daughter was a romantic soul. What had been the use of the trousseau, so meticulously prepared and the 'French-style' wedding gown, that she wore only on the second day, after interminable debates? What had her tongue-tied shyness and her purity led to?

I recall these scattered details of that wedding celebration – the copulation on a rush-mat, an unloving bridegroom and a tear-stained bride – but I also remember the bitter prelude, the outburst which some will deem puerile. As if, in our town as elsewhere, whether the marriage is celebrated with the blessing of a long-dead saint or accompanied by shrill cries of jubilation from submissive towns-women, there was no hope in sight thereafter.

# 7

# REST BY THE WAYSIDE

I do not know why I am conveying this cascade of misery, I do not know why the bodies of these women always precede me on my journeyings, why I find them lying across my path, casting their dark shadows, they who have travelled the rough road of their daily lot, spurred on only by the hope of bliss.

There is no vista of blue skies, here where I speak my hesitating words, where protest is silenced. The women's wombs bring forth children, their arms are never still, their faces bend low over the fire to stoke the flames under steaming cauldrons. Groups of children stand around, their fretful cries cast streaks of jangling sound across the sanctuary of the fleeing soul.

As for the man who leaves the house, who comes and goes, who enters to give orders, insisting on the low table being laid, the man, all men – they batten on us, fed every day from our overflowing hands, fed on our anguished voices while our patience reaches breaking point, then, as every night approaches, we must submit our weary bodies to them, bodies that yearn for the moment of peace, for the calm lake of prayers before the final descent into the ground.

Boys hanging on their mothers' breasts yesterday, or yesteryear, and who become aware of their maleness as soon as they are weaned. Another child is on the way, to be delivered by this same body in a crater of silence – and with the tenacity of a leech or octopus. The first son, the second and the third no longer suck at the milk-swollen breasts; but they prowl around, begging for the maternal warmth, first cooled and then denied them. They are never far away, these precocious males, even when husband or lover of another woman. They wait for the mother's body to be put in the ground and then find peace, but why? Oh, Allah's Messenger, you who scarcely knew your mother, could you dwell in the heart of that secret, that bitter cactus?

Nurturing sons by day, husband by night, so that they alone may enjoy the broad light of day! Nurturing them tirelessly, tying a permanent knot so that we can hold them in check by invisible reins. To this we come, after our destined travail in a cloistered void.

Eventually youth passes from muscles, skin and hair. Ten, twenty years slip by, in the confines of a hovel, or maybe on a spacious patio where fountains play and caged turtledoves coo. Respite comes: the husband will take a co-wife; Oh, to feel free at last, to be really independent – a queen! The sons wish for virgins, whom we shall have to choose for them, running our hands over prospective brides in one of the local *hammams* – as if, fearing to bring home a rival, the child-man requested this contact with maternal fingers so that he alone could then strip away innocence.

Yes, respite intervenes. Life can begin at forty, or at sixty. We can drop off to sleep with a rosary in our fingers; sit down and be waited on: talk, giving orders, calling down blessings or curses, but still talking, like a ship adrift in the ocean! Sitting in judgement on the kingdom of women.

Five times a day, in exchange, delighting in wrenching the body apart, head down, head up, inclining, unfolding, contracting, prostrating, fragmenting, duplicating, triplicating the body, five times a day, this body that begets no more, no longer gives suck, no longer lends itself to blind embraces, five times the forehead touching the cold floor, face on the worn wool of the rug, crouching on bare heels, body flattened on the ground, prone, recumbent, arched, raised, straightened up, five times a day, to mumble that one and only love, letting it penetrate elbows, knees, skull, every vertebra of the buttressed back, every henna-ed finger joint, five times a day! Prostrate in front of Allah and his Prophet, the body finds ease, far from men, far from the man, the cascade of litanies intrudes on the texture of the interior cooing voice. The mosque is filled with the scent of rose-petals, jasmin, myrrh and incense. Contemplate the temple after the women have left. There is a lilac freshness in the air, that you can drink in like absolution after sin.

Roaming every morning through the alleys which have been waiting for us since that day when, as little ten-year-olds, we were decreed to be women and so must be shut away! And now these narrow streets are ours again; as we trip along, they are awash with pearly mauve light, and their dusty haze trembles on the horizon. We trot along the alley-ways that belong to us once more, our veils no longer veils but items of adornment. Would it not be us, returning to the street?

Contemplate the house filled with daughters-in-law, children, sons who return home in the evening and in the morning kiss our hands and leave again.

Sitting musing, calling on the Prophet and his saints, listening to invisible fountains which quench our thirst, we gaze serenely on the whole household. The body, shrouded in crêpe or light velvets, can slip away.

Praise be to God and may he call us soon! Death will be a release.

# 8

# A YOUNG GIRL'S ANGER

So childhood days slipped past. The matriarchs, our guardians; vigilant statues. The grandmother's formidable presence, seated there. My mother's mother.

That patio, retreat for women in waiting. I left it when I was ten or so. Was that really 'my' home, 'our' home? It was certainly home for my grandmother, and the other women. Although deprived of every right, they held court in these courtyards. They thought themselves queens of the harem, when in truth they had only walk-on parts.

My father returned from his long absence to take me away from my aunt who had brought me up till then, so finding consolation for producing only sons – oh, proud indeed the mother of many males, but what arid future lies in store for the woman who has had no daughters to rear! . . .

I continued my studies in the capital. To do so I had to be a boarder; a few exceptional girls like myself, spared from a life of seclusion, while still haunted by its proximity or its threat, felt themselves doubly alienated from their European schoolfellows, the daughters of colonials settled on the plain.

My aunt had hidden neither her tears nor her helpless distress at my departure.

'Study?' she had muttered. 'Is she a man? . . . Alas! Everything is changing nowadays, everything is upside down!'

And she blamed the 'law of the *Roumis*'.

'Yes, I'm putting her to school with the *Roumis*, as you say! But she will return to you afterwards,' my father promised.

She accused her own brother of robbing her of her 'mother's hopes', thus implying that her own sons, on becoming 'men' would no longer be her sons.

As for me, I dreamt of boarding-school as of some exotic land.

Those last summer afternoons slipped by one by one, in that ground-floor courtyard. Translucent hour with women posing, still as statues: coffee, pastries, idle chatter. Sad cage-bird-women. Families connected to us by marriage lived on the first floor: cousins and their wives whom I've never seen since. The women all came down for this afternoon break, each carrying her copper tray and sweetmeats, to partake of coffee or tea, and quince preserves prepared in the traditional way.

I remember one cousin who looked like a village woman. Her husband was in financial difficulties: a shop on the verge of bankruptcy, some transactions in cereals which had apparently gone wrong. They were staying there temporarily, for one or two seasons, before leaving the town; the man was hoping for a job with the railways. There was talk of a post some way away, in a small town to the east.

The couple had seven or eight children. The woman was secretly nicknamed 'the broody hen', not because of the size of her family, which was fairly commonplace after all, but because of the short intervals between her pregnancies. Her eldest daughter was fifteen, or sixteen at the outside!

Houria – that was the latter's name – was just about to become engaged. The parents quarrelled every evening: the father wanted to 'give' her and the mother stood out against this.

'She helps me look after the little ones!' she grumbled as she sampled the pastries. 'There are three boys after her. How shall I manage all alone, here I'm pregnant again, and it's barely a month since I weaned the youngest!'

She spoke almost with detachment; even a hint of satisfaction, as if from force of habit. She seemed to be commenting on the inevitable fate of an alien body.

These are the exact circumstances in which – yes, twenty years later, it still echoes in my ears – Houria turned on her too compliant mother, and twenty years on, the sharp edge of that tremulous, immature voice suddenly pierces my memory.


Was it some young aunt or a temporary servant who, long ago, during a childhood siesta, whispered to me the secrets of the nightly goings-on among that innumerable brood?

Their bedroom was lit by a central oil-lamp and there the mother and eldest daughter put down the mattresses, side by side. The father lay at one end, the mother at the other. The seven or eight children squashed in between under the same blankets; they were separated according to sex: the adolescent daughter slept beside the mother, with the little girls next to her and the boys on the other end of the row.

The lamp was put out. The father reeled off his *shahada* out loud, making the youngest children do likewise, under the pretext that he had to supervise the correct Quranic pronunciation. The children intoned the vague sing-song; most of them fell asleep very quickly afterwards. One of them even began to snore; the mother was the last to finish the evening prayer as she had to catch up with all the ones she'd been forced to omit during the day, because of her domestic duties; finally she too lay down with a few groans.

About half an hour later, when the room was filled with the warmth from the sleepers' bodies and the murmur of their regular breathing, a signal was given: the father grabbed his Moroccan leather *babouche*, placed on the carpet near his hand, and tapped three times, quickly and insistently.

Silence; the fifteen-year-old, who was not asleep, lay very still, waiting, her whole body tense. The father repeated the signal more peremptorily, a second, sometimes a third time.

The mother got up, groped her way across the room to her husband on the other end. And returned to her place some time afterwards, when once he had done with the fun and games he had demanded so imperatively.

One day, the adolescent admitted to someone (perhaps to this aunt whom I've lost sight of, or the temporary servant who got married in her turn in a similar room) to the pattern of the nights, regulated by the master's call to the enslaved or consenting mother. In what bitter, vindictive tone did Houria broach the subject? How far did her confidences go? I never learned; I never asked. In any case, a voice — I can still hear it in the stillness of the siesta — described to me the ritual prelude to copulation.

Until the day when, in a pause during these gatherings on the patio, the girl challenged her mother in front of us all.

The women must have been teasing the latter when she first confessed, blushing with embarrassment, 'Alas! I'm pregnant again!'

'What! your youngest isn't even one yet!'

'The bottle's to blame,' another intervened. 'Since you prefer milk in a bottle to that which the Lord provides, you have a baby every year! You might be living in a cowshed!'

'No! the man's to blame! He's never satisfied!' another one retorted sharply.

She went on to accuse the husband of the 'broody hen'. Wasn't he reputed for his 'love' of children, if the way he put up with the racket they made every day was anything to go by?

Suddenly, the fifteen-year-old virgin stood up and pointed her finger at her mother in the middle of the gathering.

'No! It's all your own fault, Mma! You're the only one to blame! You could just refuse to get up and hurry over to the man when he bangs his slipper on the floor to call you every night!'

Houria burst into tears, some of the women would say later, 'for shame'; she ran off from the group, left the patio to take refuge in one of the bedrooms. A heavy silence fell; the mother wept silently, like a meek sacrifice. The women, frozen-faced, exchanged glances, foiled of their chit-chat. One of them said in a shocked whisper, 'She called her father "the man". Oh the Lord preserve us!'

Total amnesia has swallowed up the rest of the scene for me. As if I had been rooted to the ground at first, and then had walked away . . . As if I had not the heart to define my own disquiet.

Only today can I reveal the nature of my reserve: there is a throbbing ache within me, as if from some deep bruise. It was not Houria's lack of modesty which shocked me, nor even the picture of all the children lying side by side in this cosy juxtaposition of bodies. What I could not accept was the girl's blazing outburst of stark hatred, expressed towards the too-submissive mother.

# 9

# THE SWING

When I was a teenager I was always reminding myself that my father had delivered me from the harem. In later years, I stayed away, roaming the world, as long as possible.

Every day, in every street of every town in which I might happen to be. Ever walking and ever in love. The sun would look down on me. As I roved, with an insatiable appetite for the wind, new prospects and fresh skies, I forgot the times of meals, an important appointment, some humdrum sedentary task. The intense light made me inveterately absent-minded. At other times, at the slightest step, I had to be careful not to break into a run, as if I was in danger of taking off. A time of joy and gladness, when, at the slightest incentive, you feel you can cleanse your soul in the fresh radiance of the day. Then night falls, brimming over with transparency. Oh! sometimes I feel as if I had been twenty for twenty years!

Eventually, I left the man I thought I loved. I was surfeited; or had been exposed to too much sun. I forgot him straight away. Only now, long after we split up, I realize that it was essential for me to disburden myself: what primal injury risked reappearing?

There was that long-gone day when, suddenly, the door slammed closed on my childhood for ever.

We little girls never ventured into the European districts, at the foot of the new town. But I was lured by a distant market, up against the town walls: it resembled a caravanserai, with peasants and farmers bringing throngs of animals, donkeys, mules, horses on the same day every week. The women who sold hens, quails, eggs, were pure Berber in appearance (indescribably piercing green eyes, long faces, aquiline noses, golden or tawny hair, most often dyed nearly scarlet with henna) which made them seem to me romantic and proud. And that smell compounded of carob-beans and manure, in clouds of dust!

One of my young boy-cousins, a playmate and fellow-conspirator, led me there by a roundabout way. Beyond an embankment stretched the characterless district of modern villas with its exceptional view over the harbour. This isolated market was the only reason for our surreptitious visits to this place.

One day, this cousin and I ventured 'beyond the raised ground which was the limit for the caravanserai, in the direction of the main street that glittered with neon lights. 'It's a fun fair!' my cousin whispered. Suddenly bursts of music began to grind out: the blare of a band, the nostalgic wail of an accordion washed over us. We were being carried along in completely new crowds.

I don't know how we discovered, among the booths, a most exciting attraction: to one side, in the semi-darkness, swings had been set up. Which one of us found the necessary money? Probably the cousin who must have borrowed a coin from one of his school friends whom he'd just greeted.

So we went, two intimidated but determined children, to buy our tickets. To wait our turn, to climb into the huge metal swing, facing each other. Up till then the mechanism had been stationary; but when it was lifted up into the air, when, as I sat trembling but entranced, tightly gripping the bars, I felt my body rise and dance to the regular rhythm, nothing else existed, neither the town, nor the crowds, nor my cousin, only the motion of space and myself swinging to and fro.

Potency of those next minutes. The confused din down below: the barker's voice announcing the end through the tannoy; the plangent, insistent strains of the accordion, the tumult – distant yet so near – seemed to arise from a country to which I'd never return.

The better to feel the rush of the wind against my cheeks and quicken the excitement which was making me feel weightless, as if I was being scattered in pieces into the early evening, I had stood up. I was enjoying myself bending my knees and letting my pleated skirt whirl around me, when the swing began to slow down. My cousin sat there still, his eyes riveted on me, and was shouting something over and over again; I couldn't hear anything, and I couldn't care less.

He looked scared; he was still frightened when the machine first

135

came to a halt and I finally caught the note of panic in his voice. 'Your father!' he kept saying.

This time the swing gradually approached the ground. I saw my father in front of the crowd of men. He was looking up with an inscrutable expression on his face and he was waiting; he was waiting for us. I hadn't time to be afraid. My heart was still beating fast from the exhilaration of being so high up in the air.

My cousin, who feared a scolding, jumped down, sneaked away on the opposite side and disappeared into the darkness. Unperturbed, my first concern being to rid myself of that prolonged intoxication, I advanced with a smile.

I had time to think, 'He'll excuse my escapade or he'll punish me.' A minute slipped by. Wasn't the main thing to understand – even if not straight away – why the body felt weightless at a high altitude?

My father seized my arm, gripping it as if in a vice. Without uttering a single word, he propelled me roughly away from the crowds.

'We'll go back home together!' he finally rapped out, in a cold, threatening voice.

The night enfolded us. His hand still gripped my arm. As we reached the deserted alley-ways of the Arab district, he began to speak in a hollow voice as his anger gradually flared up. He seemed to be talking to himself. And I became aware of my bitter disillusionment.

When I finally caught the words he was muttering, I found I was listening to a stranger, not my father; 'no, not my father' I kept telling myself. A man was walking beside me, carrying on a soliloquy. I only half understood: what shocked him was neither my cousin's escapade, nor my disobedience. I slowly came to the conclusion that it was the fact that 'his daughter, his own daughter, dressed in a short skirt, could show her legs to all those men staring up at her, down below!'

His daughter was showing her legs. Not me, I didn't enter the picture, but some ghost which was practically obscene! For my part I just listened, I gave up trying to break away from him. 'His daughter . . .'

All the way home, I had the feeling I was walking through those narrow passage-ways, close to a man who was tipsy, like those

136

beer-drinkers that the women so despised.

My punishment, when we got back, was simple. For several days, I was not allowed to join my father for meals. My grandmother, who brought me my food, asked no questions. The younger women relatives, on the other hand, shrieked with laughter when my cousin told them what had happened. I was however very careful not to betray the language that my father had let slip. I was ashamed, or frightened, for his sake. I was so concerned for him to retain his halo in their eyes at least, if not henceforth in mine.

That day, I left my childhood behind for ever; my father's words had projected me into another world, higher than the fairground swing, or into the depths of a strange abyss. Shortly afterwards I left the town where I was born and spent the first years of my adolescence in a boarding-school where daughters of colonial settlers – gilded youth – were in the majority. I thought I had forgotten the disillusionment of that evening.

My unusual situation as an 'emancipated' Arab girl needed a firm anchorage. I loved my father with a joyful and grateful heart. I kept telling myself that he had delivered me from the harem!

It was with difficulty that I discovered the truth: my father was at the best only the organizer of premature funerals.

*Childhood, O Hajila! I must unearth you from this mouldering heap under which you have been buried. Fragments of scenes from former times rise to the surface; they are washed up on the shores of this story as it runs its course. And I hunt for a way to introduce myself to you, since in other people's eyes you are – or perhaps it is I who am – the co-wife, the interloper, the woman who spells danger. Before continuing our story, I must find the source of all these sighs, I must discover the lacerations hidden in the depths of the soul.*

*Childhood, O Hajila! Dawn overflows from the teeming havoc, the raucous voice of the anonymous singer trails out from the taverns. Her caged song denounces the saccharine of all exoticism: seraglios of silence and of mourning.*

*Isma, the impossible rival, haphazardly weaving a story to free the concubine, hunts for the ashes of a past that has gone up in smoke. Is this woman who is speaking, whose dreams have been burnt up by memory, really me, or some ghost within me, who steals in, sandals in hand, and mouth gagged? To waken her sister to what disillusionment . . .*

# PART III

## THE SULTAN'S BRIDE LOOKS ON

*La lune était sereine et jouait sur les flots*
*La fenêtre enfin libre est ouverte à la brise*
*La sultane regarde.*

VICTOR HUGO, *Les Orientales, X,*
Clair de lune, *1828.*

*And what if Scheherazade were to be killed at the break of every day,
before she could lift up her story-teller's voice?*

*What if her sister, whom she had installed as a precaution under the
bridal bed, had fallen asleep? What if the sister had thus relaxed her guard
and the sultan's bride for one night had been delivered up to the
executioner, waiting in broad daylight, with his axe?*

*What if, when Scheherazade disappeared, voiceless, she in her turn took
her place under that same bed of love and death, which was transformed
into a story-teller's throne, and what if a second sleepless sister forgot her
task again? What if this one neglected to keep watch, neglected her duty to
wake her sister, prepare the strategy and ensure the sole road to salvation?*

*What if this first lapse were the root of our first misfortune?*

*What if, at every present and future dawn, once or a thousand and one
times, every sultan, every beggar, who is a prey to the ancestral fear that
leads to violation, were still satisfying his need for a virgin's blood?*

*Yes, what if Scheherazade were to be continually reborn, only to die again
at every dawn, just because a second woman, a third, a fourth, did not take
up her post in her shadow, in her voice, in her night?*

# 1

# THE MOTHER

Touma, the mother, is sitting in the kitchen, on the tiled floor, on a straw mat or white sheepskin which is concealed beneath her ample form and light, all-enveloping clothing. The mother sits rooted there. Like an uncut block of marble set up in readiness for the sculptor's hand, facing me when I enter, after I've rung the front-door bell. I find myself once more in the long room, into which the morning sunlight streams. The bay window at the end looks out on to a yawning chasm.

I have to stoop down to brush the lady's one shoulder, then the other with my lips. Then we tentatively let our fingers meet: a courtesy benediction. The boy who opened the door for me and showed me into the passage stays in the background. He offers me a chair.

Now I too am seated, perched high above Touma. That doesn't make her seem any lower to me. On the contrary. She doesn't have to reach up or stretch her neck, nor meet my gaze defiantly. She sits quite still; imperceptibly on her guard.

Redoubtable naked athletes, with tongues cut out and testicles crushed, in breastplates of copper and gold, armed with scimitars, used to guard the entrances to the seraglio. Ensuring perpetual watch.

Behind them, female bodies, buried in scarlet silks and velvets, are curled up on divans, strewn with pearls, feathers and gold, booty dumped in random heaps.

In former times, every master with his janizaries was killed by the next master, who posted the same eunuchs at the gates of the harem. The cloistered concubines, like ripening fruits, watched empty-eyed their beleaguered days slip by . . .

Now, the mothers keep guard and have no need of the policeman's badge of office. The seraglio has been emptied, but its noxious emanations have invaded everything. Fear is transmitted from generation to generation.

The matriarchs swaddle their little girls in their own insidious anguish, before they even reach puberty.

Mother and daughter, O, harem restored!

'I've come to find out when my daughter's father will be back from his trip . . . Meriem would like to see him before we leave the capital!'

'I recognize you,' Touma replies, after studying me carefully. 'May salvation be with you, once more!'

I wait. Will a curtain of stock ceremonious civilities flap between us? The white glare of summer heat fills the room, blurs our outlines.

With a low table in front of her, on which she has just spread·an embroidered cloth, Touma begins to pour the coffee. I'm still waiting.

Silently, agile as a young kid, Nazim comes to squat at my feet. The mother glances quickly at the child; I wonder if he understands her crude Arabic which lacks the refined accent of the cities. The intense light splashes and spills over him, making him a ghostly figure; he appears to be deaf to our murmured exchanges.

'I recognize you!' Touma repeats. 'When you came last year, with the local match-maker, you said you were looking for a wife for a relative. But it was for your own husband, and you were choosing a co-wife!' (Because this word means 'wound' in Arabic, I thought I heard the echo: 'You were choosing a wound!')

'I was not lying! Can a ten-year-old's father become a stranger overnight? He was in fact a "relative"! . . . And there was no "co-wife": I had left the man months before you saw me. I was choosing a second mother for my daughter.'

'All the same, if I'd known that, I'd never have agreed for my Hajila!' she insists.

She hands me a cup of scalding coffee in podgy fingers whose tips still bear faint traces of henna. I do not thank her. I drink it unhurriedly; a dull torpor steals over me – why do I need to rake up the vanished past? Nazim creeps nearer to my exposed knees.

145

Touma languidly passes him a cake; he takes it, keeps it in his hand. A conventional code of conduct is being enacted as if it were a spectacle.

In the ensuing silence I can hear the lady sipping her coffee. Then she suddenly comes to life: 'Have you come back for the man? I warn you: now that Hajila is a married woman, she's the mistress of this house; I'll defend her home myself, for the sake of the children that she'll have! Besides,' she adds with a snigger, 'Hajila knows that no matter what man fate has in store for you, whether it's a sultan or a street-porter, he remains the pillar of your home!'

I return her gaze, heavy with suspicion. She suddenly stirs her massive bulk. As if she had decided to get up, and then changed her mind. She must be saying to herself, 'War? Will it be war?'

'For my part, I'm quite happy not to have a home any more! I travel light through life' (I cut short the confidences on which I'm about to embark). 'I heard of Hajila's illness. I pray she will be better soon! I only came today because of Meriem: we shall be leaving soon.'

'My daughter is resting in her room! She's a little better.'

Touma nods to Nazim. He gets up, undecided rather than apprehensive. Not knowing whose side to be on, that of the visitor, or of the woman in charge of the place.

From earliest childhood males learn to detect the breach in our defences caused by indecision – the moment of weakness which, in a flash, sets women in wrangling confrontation with each other.

What they see as children will serve to slake their appetites as adults. To widen eventually the gap between us. With their bodies, their sex, their perfidy! Forcing us more and more to lose hope. With our laughter and tears both stifled, we are adrift despite our love of life . . .

The boy is leaving the room; Touma orders him sharply, 'Go and tell Hajila to come and greet the visitor! She's well enough to get up!'

He's gone. I stand up. Shall I comment ironically, 'You give your orders everywhere and to everyone! You have found your power strengthened! It doesn't work with me!' And I begin to think, passionately, 'No tattooing will ever mark my brow or chin! I never knew my mother, so she could not pass on her fears to me!'

'I will go and greet your daughter myself,' I declare coldly. 'Besides I know my way here!'

Wasn't I the one who rented this flat before the man arrived with the children? The one who arranged the bedroom for Meriem and her brother, who ... You are lying down in that room now, the place of innocence, the room that could not be soiled by the drama. You must have wanted to take my daughter's place.

Because, as she had already left, she would never know ...

I appeared in the doorway. Standing before you, at last. For the first time. You, my daughter and my mother, my half-sister; my reopened wound (so words never lie). Supporting yourself against the wall, in your pale-blue summer dress, you try to stand. I could have wept to see your weakness.

'As soon as you're better, ask to go to the nearest *hammam*. I'll be there every Friday!'

I whispered hurriedly. Nazim is at my side. Did he understand? He'll not give anything away. I gaze at you for a moment. I was about to smile, I was about to weep. I quickly turned on my heels.

With laughter, with tears. The women of the seraglio, sultan's bride or serving-maid, face each other, meet each other's eyes ... With laughter, with tears! The sun shines through the glass pane of the skylight, high up in the prison.

The mother is standing waiting for me in the vestibule, near the front door. Her expression is inscrutable.

'Remain in peace! I shall not come here again!' I say softly. 'May salvation be with you all!'

This time I greet her without stooping down; I brush her shoulder, then her head with its complicated, many-coloured head-dress, with my lips.

# 2

# THE TURKISH BATH

I return to the fountainhead, taking refuge in the antechambers of yesteryear, in the steam room where my childhood is preserved. I thought to put the clock back. To bask again in the warm solace of murmuring voices that reverberate in high vaulted chambers.

I did not really expect you to be there. I had said 'Friday' at random; the day of public prayer. For my part, if I were to pray, it would be naked like this at the baths, my body soaking wet, dripping with sweat. Only in clouds of scalding steam, can I let go. I can only let myself be submerged in mother liquor: yesterday, that of sensual ecstasy, today the rivers of my remembered childhood.

To near that moment in every recognition when the current flows between us. No need to speak, no need to say 'you' or 'I'; just to peer into each other's face through the moist, steamy air. The day is engulfed, noon is diverted to let us enter a luminous night. We are drawn closer together by the halo of vapours that rise from the hot tanks, to be reflected in the moisture oozing from the stone. Mirrors, suppressed in the world outside by the slightest rapid glance, reappear in the recesses of these misty chambers.

*Hammam*, place of respite or amaranthine garden. The sound of water obliterates the walls, bodies are liberated under the wet marble. Every night the Turkish bath serves as a dormitory for country-folk in transit and so becomes a harem in reverse, accessible to all – as if, in the melting-pot of sweat, odours and dead skin, this liquid prison becomes a place of nocturnal rebirth. And of transfusion. Here, women can communicate by signs; here, a split-second glance, a barely perceptible touch, will seal their secret collusion.

148

Every afternoon, the place is full of wailing children, delighting in the sound of their own tears; their mothers gasp for breath, then sigh with satisfaction; virgins let slip their tunics accidentally or by design, revealing a glimpse of naked flesh to admiring eyes; matrons submit to the ministrations of the elderly masseuse, who, with her highly painted face, alone among the bathers hints at the deceptive sweetness of death.

I am in search of the source of my misgivings, of my earliest uncertainty, of my aphasia; hoping we two could meet. The children's grizzling distracts me: here more than anywhere else, motherhood asserts itself, shutting out the rest of the world.

As the sessions draw to a close and the hot room empties, when the attendant puts down her cans of water, and lies down on the marble massage slab for a breathing space, all sounds seem to hang high in the air under the cloudy vaulting; the last bathers, asleep on divans in the entrance, are metamorphosed into insubstantial sheep pausing on their way to new dream-world pastures. I splash the last cold water over myself, lending an ear to this rustling emptiness. I imagine myself at one and the same time a child and an old woman. The beginning and the end.

The voices of the day's visitors – drawn-out sighs of fatigue, brief bursts of laughter echoing and re-echoing – fill the solemnity of this monastery: hum of talk, shadows coiled up, furtively.

In this twilight realm, we meet again.


If two women – or three or four – who have shared the same man (for months, or years, or a whole lifetime, for what really hurts in this so-called sharing is the length of time it lasts) are really to come face to face, it can only be if they are naked and unadorned. At least, if physically naked, they can hope to hear the voice speak true; and then to hear the heart's truth.

Lotus-lily of memory: I see myself again as a young daughter-in-law, on my first visit to the Turkish baths in that city, accompanied by the man's mother.

Her fifty years sat heavily on her, but her face was free from wrinkles, her features scarely blurred by age. We went together into the hot room; we washed ourselves.

And I was carried back into my childhood, when the *hammam* fostered my collusion with my aunt: we would leave the hot room together, crimson-faced, holding out our hands as if bearing offerings, mellow with love.

Seated beside my husband's mother, I came near to experiencing that same emotion when she glanced up at me from the stool on which she squatted. I must have let my tunic slip down to my waist. I was combing the lather through my dripping hair, with one arm raised, my cheeks on fire. She gazed at me slowly and I returned her gaze.

In this split second I suddenly read her unease: to be sure, she was contemplating my youthful body, scarcely emerged from adolescence (and as she was devout and serious-minded, her awareness of an unspoilt beauty no doubt led her thoughts to God . . .); but I also understood that in my image she saw the reflection of her own son's desire, rekindled every night.

I pulled my tunic up to my armpits. We went on washing without another word, united by a different bond from that which links mother and daughter.

Two women, on either side of that ambiguous frontier – a man's presence.

Hajila, I was not necessarily expecting to see you there in the *hammam*. The first week I went on Friday, but also two or three days later.

On Fridays there is a very noisy crowd in attendance: it's the day for public prayer, but it is also the day when the schools are shut. During the earlier part of the day at least, children are all over the place, from infants up to little boys under seven – those who are not yet circumcised – but whose eyes already take in everything. They seem to be brought in bunches for some torture, or into the burning heart of some premature paradise . . .

During the last hour, after the mothers have left the bath with their children, silence falls on the oozing stones. An attendant passes to check that the water is running, that the little basins at the foot of the grey walls are clean. Reddish droplets – from the henna solution for the hair – leave a bloody trail on the tiles.

One or two middle-aged women were still washing in the overheated corners; a third was performing her ablutions in the middle, while droning out verses from the Quran. An intimidated adolescent was slowly and carefully rinsing her long, raven hair, as if it were her sole treasure.

On the second Friday, you came. You recognized me. You came to wash at the same basin. We didn't speak: I don't even remember any exchange of greetings. You did not take off your bath-tunic, which clung to your swollen belly.

Silently, I filled a copper cup with hot water and emptied it over your shoulders then your hair. You crouched down on your knees and said, 'Go on! Bless you! That does me so much good . . .'

I got up when you began your more intimate toilet: the old woman in charge of the various preparations brought you the evil-smelling, blue depilative paste.

'I've been here since three o'clock,' I apologized.

I retreated into the other corner. From time to time the weathered wooden door leading to the next room half-opened and I caught snatches of muffled sound from the other bathers, as well as the smell of oranges they were peeling. I lay down on the marble slab. Sunbeams filtered through a skylight in the centre of the ceiling, as if reaching us from some previous journey through infinity . . . I closed my eyes.

Shortly afterwards, when you had finished washing, we left this room together.

'As long as I'm in this condition,' you explained, emphasizing your words as you ran your hand over your belly, 'I can't stay here more than half an hour at the most.'

'I'll see you next Friday,' I replied and went to lie down to wait for my body to cool off before getting dressed.


By the third Friday I felt I had worked out a plan. I perfected the details once I was inside the baths. As on the previous occasions, I arrived early.

I washed slowly. I used very little water, liberally rewarding the attendant for the many cans of scalding water which she brought me. She volunteered to wash me, promising to scrub and massage me, splash water over me, give me a thorough shampoo, ending with a good rinse then wrapping me in wool, 'like a new bride' as she temptingly proposed, as if she were a procuress. I refused. I had to explain that I liked to do things in my own way: first soaking my hands, then warming up my legs and thighs and finally washing my upper body (at that point she could soap my back); afterwards I would throw back my head and shampoo my hair like a European: alas! no henna? no special powder to be rubbed into my scalp? The old woman, with the face of a laughing witch, stared at me.

'I like to take my time!' I said. 'I come and go till I've finished.'

Did I have to confess that I was there not just as a bather, but also to recapture my childhood and play once more the part of an observer? My eyes got used to the darkness. I sat down in the tepid room on one of the rough stone benches, in between mothers and children, and shared the fruit they offered me. The more the din increased, the more invisible I felt: as if I were not entirely there, nor anywhere. I listened to snatches of conversation; the warmth of the atmosphere lent words a poetic quality and nothing else in the world existed with the exception of this deep grotto.

*Hammam*, refuge where time stands still. The very concept of enclosure and thus of imprisonment, dissolves or disintegrates. Seated between two doors, between two extremes of temperature, my skin exposed by turns to the sting of icy water and scalding steam, suddenly I was aware of nothing but voices finding relief in sighs, purified of the triteness and dissonance of words. I let the sounds alone pervade me, sounds which also seemed to be washed clean. The murmur of water constantly flowing, the flickering forms and fluctuating noises around me brought on an incipient lethargy – or rather, I felt I might, as habitual bathers did, become addicted to the drug of lethargy.

*Hammam*, the only temporary reprieve from the harem . . . The Turkish bath offers a secret consolation to sequestered woman (such as organ music offered in former times to forced religious recluses). This surrogate maternal cocoon providing an escape from the hot-house of cloistration . . .

Since you had resolved to come (accompanied as on the previous occasion by your sister Kenza who did not wash but waited squatting on the mattresses in the lobby, either sleeping or chatting), I knew, this time, what I had to say to you.

We washed side by side. At one moment, we turned our backs to devote ourselves to the minutiae of our toilet. And before I had pulled my tunic up again you turned round and offered to soap my shoulders and back; you sprinkled the last lot of water over me, the coldest used for rinsing. I then did the same for you. But I was ready before you, remember.

I wrapped my long, thick towels around me, knotting one under my arms and letting it fall to my knees, covering my head and shoulders with the other. My hair was plaited and hidden under a salmon-pink satin cap.

I kept my copper cup, as was the practice. You filled it with cold water for me: once we had passed through the heavy door I poured it over my feet to cool them down.

I bent over to embrace you. The old attendant who entered at that moment thought I was giving you the customary ritual kiss on leaving the *hammam* . . . But in fact I was whispering, as if no trace remained of all the discarded debris of the past. It had all been drowned.

'Look, I've a key in my hand! Take it!' I repeated.

You took the key without understanding. I embraced you. I murmured the customary formula, then added, 'Touma prevents you going out, except for this weekly bath. It's up to you to decide whether you keep the child you're carrying, or whether you get rid of it. Get out of the house, go and consult a doctor or a friend, anyone you like. Get out for the sake of getting out!'

You stared at me, eyes wide open, the moist steam dripping from your arms. As you stood awkwardly, with an expression of childish indecision on your face, I was finally aware of your grace as a woman; your secret. (And I remind myself that in my Arabic dialect, over and above the beauty that is celebrated in a woman, she is mostly praised for her 'secret' – of which an elusive trace momentarily flashes across her face.)

'The key to the flat?' you ask in astonishment.

'I don't know why I kept the duplicate! . . . But it's your key! I shan't go to your home again, nor come to this bath in future. If you want to talk to me, ask Nazim, he knows where his sister and I will be during the summer. He's even supposed to be coming to visit us!'

'Thank you!' you reply, grasping the key.

Already the attendant approaches with her cans of water to escort me conscientiously out of the steam room.

Saturated with scalding steam, then soaked in tepid waters, finally stung with icy cold, we dread the thought of the outside world. The door gapes open, then closes quickly, but wind or hot air has already swept inside. The outside world spells cruel exposure for our softened bodies.

We muffle ourselves up, and emerge like ghosts with open eyes. Is it to retain on our bodies the breath of Eden, the sweetness of its waters?

# 3

# ON THE THRESHOLD

The following week, I started walking at random through the town. From dawn to mid-afternoon, when my daughter gets out of school. To walk back with her to my aunt's house in the *medina*. This return together is my sole aim. Up till then, the whole morning and part of the day, I wander aimlessly.

All the while I was away, I had carried with me the glare from the whitewashed walls of this city, where I had always thought myself to be prepared for anything: its thoroughfares, sometimes deserted, sometimes filled with noise, the slightly tilted façades of its buildings, but most of all, those endless flights of steps leading down steep streets (these alone, if put end to end, would form a bottomless precipice for us to hurl ourselves into oblivion!)

I had returned on an impulse, to show I had not deserted my child; I had had eyes for nothing around me. As if I were only passing through this metropolis. Whatever it may promise, nothing of my past lies hidden here except my adolescent folly, my erstwhile love. The suffocation I felt in those long-gone days has left no trace in me.

I felt myself to be in transit in this capital overhanging the sea. Was not this illusion taking me back to my origins – that distant red-brown city which my mother never left? I will make my home nowhere else.

I must never fall in love again, except in the place of my birth, in my own kingdom. I don't know what man will be my next choice, but at least I want to anticipate the setting in which I may find love.

But you have lived cooped up all your life between these steep streets with their murmurous hum, in this precariously balanced city where not just the land is in constant danger of collapse, but one's identity also threatens to cave in. This is the place from which you are trying to escape; you are looking for a way out of this prison. This city is the ship on which you first cast yourself adrift; from here, your journey will begin.

I have resumed my wandering. So I no longer call you into existence, I no longer have to imagine you. I merely wait for you.

I dreamed once of suggesting you should go away with me: get an abortion legally somewhere. But I'm afraid of any more travelling. I too want to put down roots. To wear the veil again, in my own fashion . . . To retreat into the shadows; bury myself.

On some mornings, I would go out too early. The city, pristine in its emptiness, is taken over by troops of white-veiled cleaning-women, hurrying to the office buildings which have sprung up everywhere. They babble to each other as they rush by, as if they were dreaming and walking in their sleep; like youngsters on some escapade. The districts by-passed by the buses and where only the occasional car is to be seen, are cut off from all sound.

I imagine I am advancing after the deluge at the beginnings of the world, or after a sudden shipwreck. First some pedestrians appear: a few children, isolated men, returning from their pre-dawn devotions, a solitary beggar. They walk with circumspection. The new masters, gliding past in their limousines, leave a wake of transient mystery.

As soon as daylight streams over the city, it loses the lightness of its colours, its shifting image. It now puts on the face of an enormous, dusty straggling village, swarming with night-blind creatures. The passers-by do not look as if they really live here; more like wave after wave of persistent invaders. The noise of their trampling feet rises up from the ground.

Above the street, seeming to dominate the scene which they gaze on with indifference, naked children on the balconies and women of the household, half-hidden behind their curtains, trailing an aura of impermanence.

I went out too early. To take possession once more of the open space, where trills of laughter from the past still re-echo.


On the last day, I followed you. I hung around near your building. I had no plan. I was just free to be on hand. I followed you quite openly, not surprised to see you appear. At the most, I had not thought you would go out so early.

Only your concierge stood in the doorway of your building, keeping an eye on us; he recognized me some time afterwards, he saw you – was it for the first time – 'unveiled', like a European.

As I turn when you turn, following your roundabout route, I feel I'm not only walking for walking's sake, but as a spectator. Once more I act the spy, not on you, but on the passers-by, the houses, trees, seeing them through your eyes. Looking at them for the first time.

I can tell every woman's history by the way she walks down the street: how long she has lived, what is her genealogy; I can tell if she has been around for three centuries or three days! I know if she has been wearing her hair loose and her skirts above her knees, since her grandmother was young, or in readiness for her daughter to blossom into adolescence . . . Yes, faced with any woman passing by – at least in our small towns, our *douars*, barring caves, grottos, or prisons – I have the presumption to claim that I can tell at first glance, at the very first glance, just because it is the first, where that woman is going: from shadow to sunshine, from silence to speech, from night to truth stripped bare. The first step reveals both the silhouette and the hope.

Oh, eye of the night, oh, song of love, murmured by the singer who knows no love, I conjure up the moment of liberty, by a split-second image or by a word, even in a foreign tongue.

Shall I destroy you, if I continue to address you as an intimate? I neither invent you nor pursue you. I can scarcely even testify; I simply stand here in your presence.

Although it is lunchtime, you don't even think of returning home. You must have forgotten your mother.

It is the twenty-first of March. I caught sight of the date in a stationer's window in the city, giving both that of the Christian calendar and the Muslim era . . . 'A spring day,' I observe. I blink my eyes; shreds of mist, like cotton-wool, spread through the wider avenues, nearest to the harbour. 'Spring lasts for only one day with us!' I think, as I set off again, following in your footsteps.

Turn and turn about on the world stage that is denied us, in the

157

space we are forbidden to infringe, in the flooding light that is withdrawn from us, you and I, turn and turn about, ghost and mirror-image of each other, we play both parts, sultan's bride and her attendant, attendant and her mistress! Men no longer exist, or rather, they do exist, they stamp their feet, they are everywhere, obstructing our path. They spy on us endlessly with unseeing eyes!

And then I saw you rushing headlong, hurtling down a wide flight of marble steps that led to a lower boulevard. I realized you were walking as if in a dream. I did not quicken my pace; nevertheless I did catch a glimpse of your face, as you glanced rapidly to the left, and then mechanically to the right. Children who were playing half-heartedly, like extras in a crowd scene, stared at you, you, the cranky eccentric!

I saw myself, as I had been ten, eleven years before; reminded perhaps by that sidewards movement of your head, as you reached the end of that same hand-rail, on those same steps, above that same crowded boulevard.

And I saw you leap forward. 'An antelope fleeing before the hunter,' a Bedouin versifier would begin, already searching for his rhymed banalities, his useless alliterations. You had nearly reached the opposite pavement when you were knocked down by a black car, full of laughing or angry passengers; a confused jangle of voices was heard, then the sound of hooters, then . . .

*A great shout arose (I can hear it still, as I write to you), then an outcry, then an uproar . . . ***

It took me some time to push my way through the crowd of curious onlookers and see that a woman was lying on the ground, unconscious. Two men in front of me slowly lifted her up; a third man, next to me, who seemed older, stammered,

'O Mohammed, have mercy on her! Have mercy on her, O Mohammed! . . .'

I gazed at your pale face. I saw my own face, as I had been, as I had never seen myself, at that same instant when death caresses you with his wing and his imperceptible smile seems to say to you, 'Not

---

*Quoted from the novel *Une Année au Sahel* (*A Year in the Sahel*) by Eugène Fromentin, 1859.

yet, the time is not yet right!' My own face, the face that I never discovered.

'She'll be all right!' a voice repeats, clearly upset.

I move away, I'm leaving . . . What is the use of my telling myself what I know already: that you will lose the foetus, which is already dead in your heart; and that you will live, with your yoke lightened, freed from your shackles.

The screaming siren of the ambulance draws near.

The same day I go to meet Meriem; I tell her and my aunt, who is closing up her house to go with us, 'We're leaving for home tomorrow!'

'For home?'

'For our home-town!'

The town with the ancient harbour where my journey will end is my aunt's birthplace, as well as mine. The place where the child was born, too: I had returned there when the time came for my confinement.

The second wife will repeat what the first one only half succeeded in doing: cutting her way through the same undergrowth, starting the same impromptu madness, but in the diamond-sharp light of reason.

The first one keeps secret watch and waits; lending an ear. The next step requires the same spotlights to be relit – to shed sunlight or candle glowing in an alcove. Then the first wife will vanish from the scene, fading away to be reborn elsewhere.

The sandal of liberty leaves its dancing footprints on sand or rock. In the darkness a hand or silk scarf left lying on the ground is reflected in a puddle. Eyes are opened, hearing sharpened by anticipation or encouraged by sisterly solidarity, rediscovering the warmth and the unspoilt, intuitive vision of childhood.

The second wife stands on the threshold, devouring the space: and now the first one can put on the veil, or go into hiding. The man, searching for the same wounds, gesticulates in the darkness as the day ends. The shore of morning is still.

At the end of the long night, the odalisque is in flight.

# THE LUTE

*As soon as we women are freed from the past, where do we stand? The preamble is not quite over, the queen of every dawn, on her dais, can only hope to survive for one day at a time, her salvation is only assured by every night spent in the harem, by every flight into the world of the imagination. Where then do we stand, in what wilderness or what oasis?*

*The present congeals about us. Long ago, it would yield for us, centuries before Eurydice was found by Orpheus, who lost her again, but who at least did go in search of her, did love her. You and I look with eyes that see for the first time, we feel the same distress. There is a flutter of wings up above in the dovecote, liberty is breaking out; or, more exactly, is getting ready to break out.*

*A fleeting smile on an unveiled face; can we women resuscitate our lost childhood, we who were mutilated in our adolescence, our happiness excised, cast out from the enclosing warmth of a home? The fountain gurgles in the patio . . . Where shall we find a resting-place? Our peals of laughter have faded, our dances degenerated into a confused stampede; what sun or what love will offer us stability?*

*O, my sister, I who thought to wake you, I'm afraid. I'm afraid for all women, not just we two or three, Isma, Hajila, Meriem, but all women – barring midwives, barring mothers standing guard and those carrion-beetle-matriarchs, I fear lest we all find ourselves in chains again, in 'this West in the Orient', this corner of the earth where day dawned so slowly for us that twilight is already closing in around us everywhere.*

Paris, WINTER 1981–1982; WINTER, 1983–1984; SPRING 1985 AND 1986.

# Be sure to read the companion to Assia Djebar's *Sister to Scheherazade* --

## *Fantasia: An Algerian Cavalcade*

In this stunning novel, Assia Djebar links the history of her native Algeria with episodes from the life of a young girl in a story stretching from the capture of Algeria by the French in 1830 to the War of Liberation of the 1950s. The girl, growing up in the old Roman coastal town of Cherchel, sees her life in contrast to that of a neighboring French family, and yearns for more of life than law and tradition allow her to experience. Headstrong and passionate, she escapes from the cloistered life of her family to join her brother in the maquis' fight against French domination.

Djebar's exceptional descriptive powers bring to life the lives and suffering of girls and women caught up in the struggle for independence -- both their own, and Algeria's. With its companion volume, *A Sister to Scheherazade, Fantasia* offers an authentic, many faceted portrait of Maghrebian women, past and present.